## DICKENS' NUTMEG GRATER

A nutmeg grater like this, made by Thomas Brough in 1799, was an indispensable tool of a serious punch-maker like Dickens, comprising as it does not only a box to carry the nutmegs but also a roughened surface to serve as a grater. Dickens carried this grater on his midnight rambles through the foul-smelling back streets of Shadwell, Ratcliff Highway, and Limehouse to sweeten the air.

# Convivial Dickens:

## The Drinks of Dickens and His Times

# *Convivial Dickens:*
## *The Drinks of Dickens and His Times*

Edward Hewett and W. F. Axton

*OHIO UNIVERSITY PRESS*
ATHENS, OHIO

Library of Congress Cataloging in Publication Data

Hewett, Edward, 1926-
  Convivial Dickens.


  1. Dickens, Charles, 1812-1870—Knowledge—Manners and customs.
2. Drinking in literature.  3. Alcoholic beverages.  4. Drinking customs—History—
19th century.  I. Axton, W. F., 1926-     . II. Title.
PR4592.D78H48  1983           823'.8           83-13286
ISBN 0-8214-0701-5

*To Jeanne Peltier Hewett*
*and to*
*Anne Millard Axton*

# Contents

# CHRONOLOGICAL ORDER OF DICKENS' MAJOR WORKS, TOGETHER WITH ABBREVIATIONS

| | |
|---|---|
| *Sketches by Boz* (1836): | *Boz* |
| *Pickwick Papers* (1836–37): | *PWP* |
| *Oliver Twist* (1837–39): | *OT* |
| *Nicholas Nickleby* (1838–39): | *NN* |
| The *Old Curiosity Shop* (1840–41): | *OCS* |
| *Barnaby Rudge* (1841): | *BR* |
| *Martin Chuzzlewit* (1843–44): | *MC* |
| Christmas Books | |
|     *A Christmas Carol* (1843): | *CC* |
|     *The Chimes* (1844): | *C* |
|     *The Cricket on the Hearth* (1845): | *CH* |
|     *The Battle of Life* (1846): | *BL* |
|     *The Haunted Man* (1848): | *HM* |
| *Dombey and Son* (1846–48): | *DS* |
| *David Copperfield* (1849–50): | *DC* |
| *Bleak House* (1852–53): | *BH* |
| *Hard Times* (1854): | *HT* |
| *The Seven Poor Travellers* (1854): | *SPT* |
| *The Holly Tree* (1855): | *HTr* |
| *Little Dorrit* (1855–57): | *LD* |
| *A Tale of Two Cities* (1859): | *TTC* |
| The *Uncommercial Traveller* (1861): | *UT* |
| *Great Expectations* (1860–61): | *GE* |
| *Somebody's Luggage* (1862): | *SL* |
| *Mrs. Lirriper's Lodgings* (1863): | *LL* |
| *Our Mutual Friend* (1864–65): | *OMF* |
| *Dr. Marigold* (1865): | *M* |
| *Edwin Drood* (1870): | *ED* |

# *Acknowledgments*

We wish gratefully to acknowledge the help offered by the following individuals and institutions in the preparation of this volume: the Department of English of the University of Louisville for a grant-in-aid for preparation of this manuscript, and the University itself for a sabbatical used partly for research on this book; the Martha's Vineyard School System for a leave-of-absence for research and for a sabbatical partly used for research on this book; Stanley Burnshaw, Stan Hart, Jerry Mason (and The Ridge Press), and Robert Cook of the Indiana University Press for many valuable suggestions and words of encouragement; Richard Altick, for his sympathetic reading of the MS; Mrs. Terence McHugh and Mr. H.C.D. Whinney for making photographs available to us, and Mr. Terry Pope for taking photographs; Katherine Johnson for several drawings; Mr. A.W. Noling (now deceased), of the Hurty-Peck Library of Beverage Literature, for the generous gift of his bibliography of beverage literature and the loan of many volumes from his collection; Alvin Rosenberg; the British Library; the Guildhall Library; the library of the Victoria and Albert Museum; the Dickens House Museum; the Museum of Rural Life, Reading; the Inter-Library Loan Office of the University of Louisville Library, the Office of Instructional Communications at the same place, and the Vineyard Haven Public Library; and our patient friends, colleagues, and families.

# Preface

It was when we witnessed Sarah Gamp ordering up a pint of that "celebrated staggering ale," the "Brighton Tipper," that we began the investigations which have led to this volume. We wondered what such potation could have been, and why Mrs. Gamp should have wanted that beverage above all others. The same curiosity led us to inquire about the scores of other rare drinks that Dickens specified for the creatures of his imagination: hot pineapple rum-and-water for Mr. Stiggins, warm cherry Negus for Dr. Chillip, and that memorable bowl of smoking hot Bishop shared by the newly humanized Scrooge with Bob Cratchit. Surprised to discover that this interesting subject had not heretofore received extended study, we set out to learn what the drinks of Dickens were, and how they were made; what they might have meant to him as a man and as an artist; and what they stood for in the language of Victorian social convention. Our discoveries suggested that others might be interested too.

While in the pages that follow we have tried to touch on all of these matters as occasion demands, our practical concern has been to make the drinks known to Dickens accessible to modern tipplers who might wish to savor them with some appreciation of the ambience in which they were originally enjoyed.

For this reason we have appended authentic period recipes at the end of each chapter except the first, introductory one. We have refrained from modernizing these recipes, culled from barbooks, butlers' manuals, and housekeepers' guides of the years 1820–1890, thereby imposing our tastes on the palates of our readers. Nor have we, save in the most dire extremity, ventured to offer modern substitutes that "will do as well." They won't. In most cases the ingredients of the recipes cited hereinafter can be found in cities of any size, at delicatessens, natural food or herb shops, liquor stores, grocers, pharmacies, and nurseries. In rare cases, where the original materials are simply not to be had, we have resorted to appropriate alternatives, recognizing that they are only approximations.

By the same token, our readers should understand that the recipes described in these pages do not provide a dumping ground for inferior ingredients. Many of them are the product of centuries of refinement and, while we do not think vintage wines, say, are obligatory, our personal experience confirms the verdict of our sources: the better the materials, the better will be the resulting drink. Indeed, with Dickens himself among the number, our sources could be adamantly particular about some matters. When they spoke of lemon rind, they meant only the yellow, which contains the fragrant and flavorful *zeste*, not the bitter white pulp beneath. The ingredients of hot drinks must never be boiled, lest the alcohol evaporate. They knew the difference between a tart Seville orange and its blander cousins, and understood that different kinds of sugar yield more or less sweetness and a different flavor. When they specified borage, lovage, cucumber rind, lemon balm, spearmint, verbena, or freshly grated nutmeg or ginger, that is what they had in mind and not something else. We would be well advised to follow them faithfully.

But this discussion misses one of the main points of our volume. Our tippling grandsires had no use for the precise measurements so dear to the hearts of home economists. For them a wineglass of this and a cordialglass of that, with "some nutmeg" to top off, was sufficient, just as good cooks deal in pinches and dashes and judicious sampling along the way, trusting to individual taste to arrive at a just *au point*. Making a Victorian drink was by no means a soullessly mechanical application of a formula to a collection of materials. On the contrary, the preparation of a punch or cup was commonly undertaken in company, and the ritual of making it—mixing, tasting, conferring, correcting—was an indispensable part of the convivial occasion which it was to supply. So let it be with us.

Careful readers will notice that not all of our recipes are cut from the same cloth. Many are as simple to make as a Toddy, while others are complicated affairs indeed, hedged about with instructions and precautions. Some of the differences stem from the simplicity or complexity of the drinks themselves: a Dog's Nose is nothing more than an American Boilermaker made with a shot of gin instead of Bourbon, whereas a Wassail is a celestial thing apart. Other differences, however, reflect social changes that occurred during Dickens' lifetime and thereafter. Generally speaking, the more elaborate recipes date from earlier in the last century, and reflect a more leisurely, aristocratic, and in some ways more humane style of living, when gentlemen had the time and the domestic staffs to lavish on some receipt of "Bacchus," Terrington, or Francatelli. The later recipes of the Davies brothers and Leo Engel, on the other hand, who were professional bartenders at the grand-hotel bars just then coming into fashion, were directed toward the up-and-coming "new" men lately introduced to the pleasures of the flagon by the more prosperous and democratic later years of the century. They were loath to linger over the more sociable but time-consuming beverages of the previous generation, for they were busy getting on in the world; and the American cocktail made its appearance. For those who wish to pursue the arcane researches we have stated, we have listed in the Bibliographical Note at the end of this volume, among many other things, some of the books of drink recipes from which we have culled, together with their dates of publication.

A word here may be in order about the persistent legend that Charles Dickens was too much given to imbibing from the bottle and the bowl. The truth of the matter is far otherwise. Those who knew him best unite in affirming that the poet-laureate of Victorian tippling was in life an unusually temperate, even abstemious, man. What he liked was not food or drink so much as the theatre of conviviality of which they were the essential stage properties. He fondly made fun of all its conventions—the pontifical toast, the comic song of "harmonic evenings" with its toor-rul-loo-rulls, the public wit and strong-breathed geniality—understanding very well that it was by means of such conventions that social communion might be approached. He himself was a convivial companion, an exuberant host, and an accomplished hand at the punch bowl; and his literary references to food and drink are copious and exact even for a time that set much store by supping and toping. The warm hob at home, where he sits watching the elders at their play of life, the bright fireside at an old inn, with the fire piled halfway up the chimney, friends drawn close in a circle around a fragrant, steaming pitcher—and pervading all a nutrient atmosphere of affection and reassurance—such scenes were closest to Dickens' heart.

As to the drinks that should be served on different occasions, Dickens was never fastidious. Mr. Venus draws as good philosophy from his crude Cobbler's Punch as gentlemen ever did from fine claret or old Madeira; and as for Christmas cheer, it need not matter that Bob Cratchit's Gin Punch must stand in the stead of Mr. Wardle's Wassail of the good old country sort. It remains for the reader to decide for himself whether he wishes to investigate these old recipes in an antiquarian spirit or take the Dickensian spirit and let the spirits go. For as Mr. Venus rightly observed, a drink depends not on mere chemistry but upon the spirit that is put into it. And that, after all, is the best sort of recipe to follow.

# Chapter One

# "WoT LarX!"

Charles Dickens' artistic life began and ended in celebrating the pleasures of the flowing bowl and the groaning board. His first published sketch in 1832, "A Dinner at Poplar Walk," opens on a comfortable bachelor's breakfast, pauses over an evening brandy–and–soda, and reaches its comic catastrophe at a dinner party. The last scene that Dickens wrote before his sudden death in 1870 at the age of 58 recounts the preparations for breakfast of another bachelor, Dick Datchery. What he might have eaten is, alas! locked in the eternal silence of his creator's death; but the last word Dickens put to paper was "appetite." In between Mr. Minns and Dick Datchery, Dickens' abundant imagination breathed life into well over two thousand characters during an active writing career of nearly forty years, most of whom are depicted enjoying the table and tankard.

When the novelist was a boy, gentlemen in gaiters still sat over their Rum Punch and churchwardens in the cosy, warm taprooms of coaching inns, where Old England lingered as though it would never pass away. By the end of the novelist's life a half–century later, the old inns and their sociable inhabitants were gone, together with the colorful coaches that had served them, swept away by the coming of the railroads and other profound causes of change in the fabric of English life. In their place arose those recent French importations, the restaurant and the metropolitan hotel (the latter often a hollow, drafty affair fronting a rail terminus), and that creature of native English origin on every slum corner, the gin-palace, with all its tawdry splendors of flaring gas lamps, plate glass, and stucco neo-classicism.

But Dickens perceived that, despite the wealth, power, and sheer magnitude of the new industrial world rising around him, some invaluable ingredient of the English spirit had been lost along the way, an ingredient that had been essentially tied to the robust days of careening coaches, key-bugles, galloping teams, and inviting country inns and city taverns. The "new" men like Podsnap, Veneering, the Tite Barnacles, and their ilk, who came bobbing in the wake of industrialism and empire, led cramped, mean lives, in which the pleasures of eating and drinking were joylessly yoked to the wheel of ostentatious display. In reaction to the contrary pull of these impressions, Dickens spent his life as a writer alternately trying to recreate imaginatively that sense of humane sociability and solidarity which had marked the lost days of his youth, and satirizing the absence of these qualities in the England of his adulthood. In between these concerns, however, he always kept a sympathetically amused eye on those little social rituals of food and drink which give meaning and value to the lives of ordinary people.

Dickens was well aware of the fact that every activity of the daily life of Victorian England was tinctured by the social implications of eating and drinking. But Dickens' first loyalties lay with the ebullient world of the old coaching days, which he had known as a boy and which he knew was passing away even as he was writing his earliest works: the lusty, liquid setting of the open road, coaches and post-chaises, affectionate domestic kitchens and parlors, and steamily convivial country inns and city taverns.

Indeed, in *Barnaby Rudge* (1841), The Maypole Inn, Chigwell, becomes an epitome of all that was best in Georgian England, all that was sociable, sane, and enduring, as opposed to the irrational, violent, and anti–social that was touched into bloody life by the anti–papist Gordon riots of 1780. Threatened by this "shameful tumult" without, the Maypole stands for England itself:

> . . . All bars are snug places, but the Maypole's was the very snuggest, cosiest, and completest bar, that ever the wit of man devised. Such amazing bottles in old oaken pigeon-holes; such gleaming tankards dangling from pegs at about the same inclination as thirsty men would hold them to their lips; such sturdy little Dutch kegs ranged in rows on shelves; so many lemons hanging in separate nets . . . with goodly loaves of snowy sugar stowed away hard by, of punch, idealised beyond all mortal knowledge; such closets, such presses, such drawers full of pipes, such places for putting things away in hollow window–seats, all crammed to the throat with eatables, drinkables, or savoury condiments; lastly, and to crown all . . . such a stupendous cheese!

> . . . . . . . . . . . . . . . . . . . . . . . . . . . . . . . . . . . . . . . . . . . . . . . . . . . . . . . .

> The profusion, too, the rich and lavish bounty, of that goodly tavern! It was not enough that one fire roared and sparkled on its spacious hearth; in the tiles which paved and compassed it, five hundred flickering fires burnt brightly also. It was not enough that one red curtain shut the wild night

out, and shed its cheerful influence on the room. In every saucepan lid, and candlestick, and vessel of copper, brass, or tin that hung upon the walls, were countless ruddy hangings, flashing and gleaming with every motion of the blaze, and offering, let the eye wander where it might, interminable vistas of the same rich colour. The old oak wainscoting, the beams, the chairs, the seats, reflected it in a deep dull glimmer. There were fires and red curtains in the very eyes of the drinkers, in their buttons, in their liquor, in the pipes they smoked.

But the Maypole was the past, and was soon to pass away forever before a mob of rioters, in an act prophetic of the slow demise of the old, stable order, and the traditional, fraternal way of life it embodied, under the rising tide of industrialism. Liberty and equality, it turns out, negate fraternity.

But then, all things relating to flagon and trencher were rapidly changing during Dickens' lifetime. Licensing laws for ale-houses were eased after 1830, so that by the time of the novelist's first big hit, the *Pickwick Papers*, in 1836, there were nearly 50,000 new ones in the kingdom, and they totalled roughly one for every neighborhood. The modern form of the pub was also evolving during the same period into its definitive three-part configuration of public bar, tap-room, and parlor or lounge. Ever emulous of the lavish new gin–palaces, the public house developed its gaudy–dowdy but comfortable blend of polished mahogany, brass, casks and bottles, red curtains, and florid glass everywhere— bevelled, mirrored, frosted, etched, and gilded with brand names—the whole dominated by a stately parade of beer-pulls. Closer to the novelist's heart, however, was the dwindling number of independent publicans and innkeepers, like Benjamin Britain of The Nutmeg Grater Inn (BL) and the immortal if obtuse John Willet of the Maypole, tens of thousands of whom once brewed their own ales and beers and presided over their own cheery hearths. The establishment of "off-license" premises (the beverages bought there had to be consumed elsewhere) and the national distribution of bottled ale allowed genteel folk to drink in the privacy of their homes, thereby further diminishing the free–and–easy camaraderie of inns and taverns, where travellers of every class had met and mingled. Even American cocktails, cobblers, and mint juleps were coming into fashion among the *beau monde*, while that cold and brittle sparkling wine, Champagne, could be found in the glass of every new–rich *arriviste*.

Inventive to a fault, the Victorians gave us both the Martini Cocktail and Temperance. While Dickens had little patience with Teetotal fanatics like his quondam friend and illustrator, George Cruikshank, a reformed drunk, and even less with militant Sabbatarians, who wished to prohibit every form of public entertainment on the workingman's only day off in the week, he knew that the Temperance movement had a point. The corner local or gin–palace was virtually the only social institution available to the urban proletarian until much later in the century. That being the case, it is not surprising that at mid-century the average Englishman spent more on drink than on rent. Per-capita consumption of malt beverages averaged more than 43 imperial gallons, that of home–distilled (i.e., English-made) spirits about a gallon, and of wine (most of it the heavily fortified Iberian kind) more than half a gallon. And these figures do not include the most popular spirits of the time, brandy and rum, which were largely distilled abroad, homemade beers and wines, and smuggled and boot–legged goods, all of which taken together amounted to a considerable additional part of actual consumption. No wonder there were so many "benchers," "brewer's horses," and "loose fish"—drunkards, in short.

While Dickens lamented the passing of tavern, inn, and coach, he was no less the man who introduced the great city of London into the novel as perhaps his ultimate subject and theme. For the teeming metropolis fascinated him as it did so many writers of the time. The following is a description of early–morning London:

> The gaslit public-houses are the first shops to open in the darkness well before dawn, especially in those teeming market areas, Covent Garden and Smithfield. In the latter, the din of whistling, barking, bellowing, bleating, grunting, squeaking, and the cries of hawkers, the shouts, oaths and quarrel-ing on all sides; the ringing of bells and roar of voices, that issue from every public house; the crowding, pushing, driving, beating, whooping, and yell-ing . . . quite confound the senses. From Southwark the great brewers' drays begin to rumble over the bridges; the quayside wharves and ware-houses are awake, where the kegs and barrels and hogsheads wait, of gin and rum and wine. The essential London, that feeds and gives drink to the whole, wakes and works long before the rest, getting ready for another day. And throughout the day to come till dawn breaks again, the sounds of people ordering meals, and being served them, and eating and drinking and being washed up after, are no small part of the great hum.

This "essential London" was never far from Dickens' mind and imagina-tion. Food and drink were to him important indices to the human qualities of individuals and to the moral texture of times and places and institutions. He knew all about the private and public lives of the host of clerks, shopkeepers, merchants, and their assistants that formed the "tide of humanity" which made its way on foot into the City every morning of the week but one from its quarters in London's inner suburbs, and made its way home every evening. Along the way, as he knew, the great arterial roads and streets were lined with taverns and pubs to minister to their thirst and hunger—as many as 46 in the three-quarters of a mile of the Strand between Trafalgar Square and St. Clement's, and 49 in a mile of Whitechapel Road. So deeply embedded in the English mind was the association of travel, drink, and tavern that the first London railway termini were given such names as The Bricklayer's Arms, The Dartmouth Arms, and The Jolly Sailor; and it was some years before more descriptive names were substituted. The old coaching days and ways, it appears, were hard to kill off.

The fact that *Pickwick Papers* opens on a bibulous meeting of the club members in a large London tavern, closes with the dissolution of that distinguished scientific body at a dinner in Osborne's Hotel, Adelphi, and in between shows the Pickwickians disporting themselves at no less than 23 inns, taverns, and hotels, is no aberration of Dickens' imagination but an accurate depiction of the central place occupied by supping and sipping in the social life of the last century. At any hour of the day or night, Henry Mayhew tells us, the streets of London were alive with costermongers shrilly hawking their food and drink to passersby and late–night pleasure–seekers. Herring and sprats, raw oysters shucked on the spot, haddock and salt cod, shrimps, mussels, cockles, periwinkles, and Yarmouth bloaters were all to be had at almost any hour of the day or night. "Cokernuts" and "pines" (pineapples)! Oranges "Two a pinny!" "Apples! an aypenny a lot!" "Here pertaters! Kearots and turnups! Fine brockelloo!" Game and wildfowl (often poached). Butter, cheese, and eggs. "Wo–or-ter–creases!" Fruit, pot–herbs, nuts and wildflowers. Each with its cry, each with its stall, barrow, tray, or wheeled stand.

At curbside one might dine off hot eels, pickled whelks, hot new green peas, and kidney pudding, while another could put together a meal of devilled marrow-bones, sheep's trotters, or mutton pie (tossing a coin with the pieman to see who paid, hence "Simple Simon"), baked potatoes, fried fish, and ham sandwiches. Fruit–tarts, cakes, buns, muffins, crumpets, and rock-candy or hoarhound drops might make dessert, with lemon–ginger ice or strawberry cream at a penny a glass. As for drink, anything but alcohol was available: ginger–beer, Persian sherbet, sassafrass tea (saloop), curds–and–whey, rice-milk, peppermint water, highly colored fizzy drinks in various flavors, hot elderberry wine, and coffee, tea, cocoa, or milk. Plain, safe, drinking water, however, was not to be had at any price.

### GINGER-BEER SELLER

One of the familiar sights among London's street-hawkers was the ginger-beer seller. He must have brewed a potent drink, for the French visitor Hippolyte Taine, whose taste of it at Vauxhall Gardens brought tears to his eyes, concluded that it must have been made of every sort of hot pepper in the world.

Eating and drinking were an off-and-on preoccupation of Londoners right around the clock, from "getting up at eight . . . breakfasting at nine, going into the City at ten, coming home at half past five . . . [to] dining at seven" for a City magnate like Mr. Podsnap (OMF)—although for his clerks and the shopkeepers getting up was earlier and coming home later, and supper for them would have been at nine. A rich merchant's breakfast was likely to have been a formidable affair served from his sideboard: cold meats, kidneys, devilled fowl, cutlets, smoked salt fish, tongue, pigeon–pie, ham, and pudding. Older–fashioned men like the coachman Tony Weller might have had cold roast beef, bread, and a pint or two of porter. Taking a "morning draught" of good hot purl at a tavern about ten or so was still not uncommon among City men who did not eat at home—for the City was an all-male enclave in those unliberated days.

For the ordinary Londoner, breakfast was more likely to consist merely of a sausage and toast cooked on the hearth at home. Cooking arrangements were still relatively primitive during most of Dickens' life, refrigeration virtually unknown, and tinned and potted foods just beginning to catch on. In most homes a single room combined the functions of kitchen, dining-room, and parlor, an arrangement that made it the center of the family's social life, as it was for Tom and Ruth Pinch (MC). The hearth, fitted out with an ingenious array of cast–iron devices to facilitate roasting, baking, and boiling, was the place where tea was prepared, meals cooked, the hot wine drinks and Wassails kept warm, and where the family gathered to enjoy them. Before the era of central heating, in short, the hearth-fire was the focus and symbol of family life. There the warmth and sustenance necessary for existence were to be found, as well as the human warmth and solidarity required for personal security and emotional well–being.

With such limited facilities, most Londoners made frequent use of the local cook–house, where roasts, hams, turkeys, and geese were baked for a penny or two, while the rest of the dinner was prepared over the hearth at home, as we see the Cratchit family doing on Christmas day. Beer and porter were brought round from the corner local by the potman. Thus on a special occasion old Sol Gills (DS) orders in a fried sole and steak, with a couple of tankards of porter, from the neighborhood tavern; and the cry of the muffin man could be heard everywhere at tea-time.

At noon laborers broke for a lunch of, say, bread, herring, and a quart of porter, which was thought to be strengthening, at the nearest tavern, while clerks and merchants waited until one. The "upper 50,000" of London, as

G.A. Sala calls them, often skimped on lunch, perhaps taking only a sandwich and a "meridian" from a pocket–flask on the run, or something more substantial at a club in St. James's or a mansion in Mayfair. But hungry clerks and shop-assistants crowded into one of the 250 or so "slap-bangs," or City chop-houses, for their mid-day meal, the most substantial one they were likely to have. The Salutation and Cat in New Gate Street or Dolly's Chop House, Queen's Head Passage, Paternoster Row, for example, were casual places with sanded floors, wooden boxes, benches, and tables, and a roaring fire at the far end—or even in the window—to entice hungry passersby. There the cook superintended "an unctuous piece of roast beef and a blisterous Yorkshire pudding bubbling hot," "stuffed fillet of beef," "a ham in a perspiration," "a shallow bank of baked potatoes glued together by their own richness," a truss or two of boiled greens, and "other substantial delicacies," as Dickens says, who is our Virgil in such greasy precincts.

Three clerks in *Bleak House* celebrate with dinner at such an "ordinary," where they take their favorite box, bespeak all the papers, insist on a full–sized "bread" and the best cuts of meat, and are "adamant in the matter of gravy." They order "veal and ham and French beans—and don't you forget the stuffing, Polly" (the waitress), to which are added three pint pots of half–and–half. As proper clerks would in a holiday mood, they go on to marrow pudding, Cheshire cheese, and a small "gargle" of rum to conclude. The bill comes to eight and six, including the usual tip to Polly—a penny from each. The Cheshire serves to remind us of the Englishman's passion for his native cheeses: no Victorian tavern worthy of its name was without its Cheddar, creamy white and blue–veined Stilton, or grindstone–sized wheels of Double Gloucester. With a biscuit or two, butter, and Sherry or Port, any one of these could make a meal in itself.

The usual dinner was a shilling and sixpence, porter, beer, or old ale included; and cook-shops, where a plate of roast beef went for as little as six- to eightpence, were even cheaper. David Copperfield ate at an alamode–beef house and paid four– to sixpence for stew or soup and bread; while soup-houses offered plain soup, bread, and potatoes for two or three pennies. Porter–houses kept a gridiron on the hearth, where customers could have their own piece of meat broiled for a penny or two, with bread, potatoes, and a pot of porter just a few pennies more. (From this institution comes the modern porterhouse steak.) And the Georgian coffeehouse enjoyed a revival in the early Victorian period: Garraway's, in Exchange Alley, was a favorite of Dickens and hence of his creature, Mr. Pickwick, who there wrote the tell–tale "chops–and–tomata-

## BUCKLERSBURY "SLAP-BANG"

London's financial center, the Old City, was famous for its fast-service restaurants, called slap-bangs because that was how the food was delivered, or "ordinaries," perhaps because that was how the food tasted. Beer and spirits were available, as well as the daily papers, and the eating was done in "boxes" like the one above occupied by the clerks Guppy, Jobling, and Smallweed. To attract customers some ordinaries had the cooking done in the window.

sauce" note to his landlady, Mrs. Bardell. Then too, many of the famous old places remained: Ben Jonson's Mermaid Tavern, beloved of Keats, Dr. Johnson's Tavern in Bolt Court, and the still–surviving Cheshire Cheese, where Charles Darnay and Sidney Carton had a fateful encounter.

## ST. CECILIA'S DAY

Victorian streets were busy places at any hour, but November's St. Cecilia's Day brought out all the street musicians, strolling bands, parades, Punch-and-Judy shows, organ grinders, circus acts, and hawkers of popular ballads. At the rear a crowded omnibus tries to make its way through the crush.

Later in the afternoon there was tea, of course—or not at all of course, for the English tea ceremony was only just coming in to general favor when Dickens was a young man and when dinner was beginning to be put off until later in the evening. But it soon became the great unifying social ritual it remains to this day, so that the parlor hearth–fire continued to be the scene of much steamy Cockney and clerical conviviality, all the more so when the teapot was augmented with a "damp" of gin or brandy, as it very often was. When Pip visits Wemmick, for example, they enjoy a "joram of tea" with the "Aged P." and Miss Skiffins, together with a "veritable haystack of buttered toast," all cooked at the hearth; and as Pip says, "it was wonderful to see how warm and greasy we all got after it" (GE).

On holidays, outings, and the new railroad excursions to Margate and Ramsgate, tea was *de rigueur*, and tea–gardens like Dickens' favorites, Jack Straw's Castle and The Spaniard's Inn on Hampstead Heath, catered to the taste, along with a little "gin–and–water–warm–with," and sprats and shrimps, afterwards. At the Temperance end of the drinking scale, tea was heavily promoted. At a meeting of the Brick Lane Branch of the United Grand Junction Ebenezer Temperance Association, the visiting toper Tony Weller is so amazed by the quantity of tea consumed (with buttered toast, ham, and muffin), that he predicts to his son Sam that "If some o' these here people don't want tappin' to-morrow morning, I ain't your father . . . There's a young 'ooman . . . as has drunk nine breakfast cups and a half; and she's a swellin' wisibly before my wery eyes."

In Dickens' time almost any occasion was reason enough to call in the local green–grocer to cater a party and to lay on a quantity of wine, brandy, hot water, lemon, and sugar. At a christening "rout" in Bloomsbury (Boz), there are dozens of extra tumblers and wineglasses in the hall, the air is fragrant with the smell of hot wine and spices, and on a trestle–table in the parlor, besides four melting barley–sugar castles and a tiny water-fountain, the boards are loaded with roast fowl, tongue, trifle, sweets, lobster salad, potted beef, rout-cakes, and bonbons. A wake might not be markedly different, as we shall see hereafter.

The River was a favorite recreational resource for Londoners, hideously polluted as it was then. The appearance of steam excursion boats in the thirties made all-day outings practicable; and Cockney families packed themselves aboard amid a welter of hampers loaded with comestibles—heavy sandwiches, wine, flat stone–bottles of cold gin punch or Negus, brandy-and-water, bottled ale and the like (*Boz*). The goal for the more well–to–do might be the Trafalgar at Greenwich (it still is), the Ship Hotel, or the Crown and Sceptre, for white-

## THE MARGATE STEAMER

August Bank Holidays brought Londoners out in droves for day-long excursions down the Thames to Margate and Ramsgate aboard the new paddle-wheel steamers. Dickens' sketch, "The Steam Excursion," chronicles the comic disaster when, as here, the sea turns rough and a party of cockney clerks and their ladies falls victim to *mal-de-mer*. Brandy and water, grog, and milk-punch were the popular topes in calm weather.

bait dinners in season between April and August. Such a dinner might begin with boiled flounder, say, followed by salmon, sole, and fried eels, after which the whitebait were brought in with a flourish. Champagne ("sham") or cold punch ("Bombo") were the usual drinks, to which Sherry might be subjoined and claret appended. After a whitebait dinner given in honor of Dickens in 1842, he wrote, Cruikshank "wound up the entertainment by going home . . . in a little open phaeton of mine, *on his head*—to the mingled delight and indignation of the Metropolitan Police." He was last seen standing on a midnight street corner, "taking gin with a waterman"—just a "kiss of the babe."

Up–river excursions were equally popular, to the pleasant rural retreat of Richmond, for example, where The Star and Garter was so well liked by Dickens that he and his wife chose it to observe their anniversaries. On the occasion of a banquet Dickens gave there, one of the guests remarked the plenitude of food and drink: "much Turtle and Venison and Lamb and Ham and Goose and at least fifty other dishes . . . Hock, Sherry, Moselle, Madeira, Champagne, Port &c . . . Ices and Creams and Pine apples, Melons and sundry other fruits." In all its prodigality of eatables and drinkables, speeches, toasts, songs, and cheers, it must have been a typically convivial evening of the sort that Dickens, and the Victorians generally, most enjoyed, and duplicated thousands of times at huge charity dinners in one of the great City hostelries.

The Victorians were also mad about sports, and such occasions as the Derby at Epsom, the Boat Races, Hampton Races, a boxing match somewhere in the country like Mousley Heath, even non-sporting events like Greenwich Fair (*Boz*) regularly attracted hordes of Londoners streaming out in their tens of thousands on foot and in vehicles to the place of action, loaded down with bulging hampers of tongue, beef, roast fowls, and ham, and liberally lubricated with milk punch, brandy, wine, gin–and–water, stout, and ale.

While the "swells," the "fancy," and the "flash mob" were pursuing these pleasures, ordinary Londoners wishing to make a night of it, like the clerks Potter and Smithers of the *Sketches*, might typically get things going on a quarterly pay–day with dinner at a chop–house in the Strand: chops, kidneys, bread, cheese, stout, and pickled walnuts, with "whiskey–and–water–warm–with" and cigars afterwards. Later, after being thrown out of their half-price seats in the "slips" (boxes) at the City Theatre for drunken rowdiness—a commonplace occurrence in Victorian playhouses—our two clerks go on to what Dickens called a "wine vaults" or "cyder cellar." Wine and cider had little enough to do with such places, as we shall see, but strong black stout did, and spirits ("breaky–leg") and cigars. The Fielding's Head in Maiden Lane (it appears in Thackeray's *Pendennis*) was famous. There W.G. Ross, dressed in sooty rags and the battered topper of a chimney sweep, first stood up to sing "My name it is Sam Hall . . . damn your eyes!" The cellars near Simpson's in the Strand were called the Coalhole, probably because its walls and ceilings were painted black in advance of their becoming naturally so through smoke and lamp–soot. Here the actor Edmund Kean founded his hyper-convivial

## WHITEBAIT DINNER "DOWN THE RIVER"

Feasting on whitebait at Greenwich or Blackwall was a feature of the "season" and summer sessions of Parliament when the whitebait, a small silvery fish deep-fried in a light batter and eaten crisply whole, were running. Accompanied by hampers of Sherry, Champagne, and claret, whitebait dinners often left the participants considerably the worse for wear. The site of "The Ship" is now occupied by the clipper-ship "Cutty Sark" but the "Trafalgar" remains.

Wolf Society; and here "Baron" Renton Nicholson later brought his scurrilous–hilarious "Judge and Jury Society" in the thirties. The latter was devoted to lampoons of current adultery cases, with the Baron as judge, aristocrats and notables in the jury-box, and the talented quick-change comic Brooks in the witness-box taking all the parts. The menu featured stewed beef hearts, rump steak, Welsh rarebits, kidneys, and "triple strength" stout.

Had saner counsels prevailed, our two clerks might instead have taken in what was by all odds the most popular form of evening entertainment in England at that time (and to some extent still is): the corner local's "Harmonic Gathering and Free and Easy," like that offered by "Little Swills and the Gentleman of Professional Celebrity" at the Sol's Arms in *Bleak House*. The

MANNERS·AND·CVSTOMS·OF·Yͤ·ENGLYSHE·IN·1849.    N°·23.

A·CYDERE·CELLARE·DVRYNG·A·COMYCK·SONGE.

The "Cider Cellar," the "Coalhole," Renton Nicholson's "Judge-and-Jury" shows, and Evanses' Supper Rooms combined to make Victorian evenings in London a riotous chorus of comic and sentimental song, where "goes" of brandy-, rum-, and gin-and-water helped wash down rumpsteak, Welsh rarebit, and devilled marrow-bones. As in the clubland of Mayfair and St James, hats were worn indoors at such all-male enclaves. To the left rear, by the piano, two "gentlemen of professional celebrity" await their turns at "Wapping Old Stairs" and "My Heart's In the Highlands."

apotheosis of a free–and–easy was Evans's in Covent Garden, which was lov-ingly described by Thackeray in *The Newcomes* and Dickens in "The Streets—Night," both of whom knew it well. Here the harmonic evening of the tavern was combined with a restaurant setting and just a touch of the music hall to come. In Dickens' little sketch (*Boz*) we are ushered into a "lofty room of spa-cious dimensions [where] are seated some eighty or a hundred guests knocking little pewter measures on the table . . . as if they were so many trunk–makers. They are applauding a Glee, which has just been executed by the three 'profes-sional gentlemen' at the top of the centre table, one of whom is in the chair—the little pompous man with the bald head just emerging from the collar of his green coat. The others are seated on either side of him—the stout man with the small voice, and the thin–faced man in black." The pompous little man in the chair is a bass, "and it is quite impossible to witness unmoved the impressive solemnity with which he pours forth his soul in 'My 'art's in the 'ighlands,' or 'The brave old Hoak.' The stout man is also addicted to sentimentality, and warbles, 'Fly, fly from the world, my Bessie, with me,' or some such song, with ladylike sweetness, and in the most seductive tones imaginable."

During an intermission, a pale–faced man with a red head asks for orders, and "demands for 'goes' of gin and 'goes' of brandy, and pints of stout, and cigars of peculiar mildness, are made from all parts of the room." Then Mr. Smuggins, who is "in the comic line," is called by the chair . . . and he "sings a comic song, with a fal–de–ral—tol–de–rol chorus at the end of each verse, much longer than the verse itself. It is received with unbounded applause"— and so on far into the night, alternating glees and goes.

The food at Evans's was no less dependable and traditional late–night fare: poached eggs and bacon, chops and steaks, steaks broiled with oysters and butter atop, devilled kidneys or marrow bones on toast, rarebits, sausages, an-chovy toast-points, and baked potatoes. The usual beverages were stout (both Guinness's and good London varieties like Reid's), bottled ale, various "half–and–half" combinations, hot brandy–and–water, Irish whiskey, hot or cold punch in season, and Negus.

Members of the "upper 50,000" might spend the evening at one of the burgeoning number of men's clubs or have an invitation to a stupefying banquet at the mansion of a merchant–prince like Dombey or Podsnap. These latter were less occasions for sociability than for display of one's wealth and powerful friends, and Dickens was merciless in his treatment of them. Weighted down with liveried footmen (the guests brought their own to help serve), heavily carved mahogany sideboards with mirrors set into them, and enormous expanses of silver epergnes, candelabra, chandeliers, and table–ware, gas lights and spermicetti candles, they remained chilly affairs at best. The food and drink offered were hardly less daunting: typically, two soups to start, then two fish, two "removes," six entrees of "made" dishes of game and game–birds, followed by a second course of two roasts, six entremets of lighter things like spinach and lobster salad to refresh the palate, then two removes of the roast, biscuit a la creme, fondues, and savories, and *then* dessert. The whole was accompanied by a variety of sherries and topped off at the end with decanters of claret, Port, more Sherry, Madeira, Sauternes, and hock, all passed "the way of the sun" (i.e., clockwise). After dessert, of course, the ladies retired to the salon upstairs, while the men stayed at the table to drink and toast, until they "joined the ladies"—if that were still possible.

For the very haughtiest of the *haut ton*, during the season there might be an invitation to the weekly ball-suppers at Almack's Assembly Rooms, King's Street, St. James's, where the food could run to sixty dishes, concluding with ices, sherbets, wafers, tea, Champagne and Rhine wine, liqueurs, cordials, and the inevitable Punch a la Romaine.

Cockneys like Jemima Evans (pronounced Ivins) and her boyfriend Samuel Wilkins might instead have headed for the Eagle Tavern, City Road, Shore-ditch, an elaborate complex of Rotunda (variety acts and vaudeville), Moorish Pavillion (drama), and Garden (an open–air dance pavillion), the whole liber-ally supplied with Negus, brandy–and–water, ale, stout, ginger–beer, rum–and–water "warm–with" sugar and lemon, Sherry, and caraway–seed biscuits (*Boz*). There were many such music halls in Victorian London.

Throughout Dickens' life London's suburbs were also dotted with "pleasure gardens." The most famous of them were Vauxhall Gardens on the Surrey side of the Thames, which dated from the later seventeenth century, and the more recent Cremorne Gardens in Chelsea. Both catered to respectable family groups in the early evening and to demi–reps thereafter, with music, dancing, concerts, discreetly shrubberied nooks, fireworks and balloon ascensions, and dubious food and drink.

For the intellectually inclined, there were "conversaziones," where one might hob–nob with the latest "lion" and have finger–sandwiches and watery Negus, as at Mrs. Leo Hunter's *fête-champêtre* in *Pickwick*. Several London taverns were given over to political debate in the evening, accompanied by food and drink and rhetoric, which Dickens satirized in "The Parlour Orator" (*Boz*).

By eleven o'clock, in the Haymarket, Leicester Square, Covent Garden,

Piccadilly and the Strand, "it is broad daylight for Bohemia," as G.A. Sala put it. Some evening parties are just breaking up, and the male guests, escorted through the streets by linkmen with torches of tarred rope, are headed for supper–rooms and after–hours houses. Others, masked and strangely costumed, are en route to a *bal–masqué*. Theaters, gardens and opera–houses are emptying, and men who have been gambling at the Wellington or playing billiards at their clubs are on their way to the Haymarket's scarlet precincts, where the streets were thick with prostitutes:

> Parties returning from the different theatres foot it through the muddy streets; cabs, hackney–coaches, carriages, and theatre omnibuses, roll swiftly by; watermen with dim dirty lanterns in their hands, and large brass plates upon their breasts, who have been shouting and rushing about for the last two hours, retire to their watering–houses . . . the half-price pit and box frequenters of the theatres throng to the different houses of refreshment; and chops, kidneys, rabbits, oysters, stout, cigars, and "goes" innumerable, are served up amidst a noise and confusion of smoking, running, knife–clattering, and waiter–chattering, perfectly indescribable (*Boz*).

The "different houses of refreshment" included hotels, restaurants, "cigar–divans" (whence the term "dive"), oyster–houses, supper–rooms, and that ubiquitous house of refreshment, the street itself, with its indefatigable vendors. By the sixties, Duborg's, The Hotel de Paris, Gatti's, the Cafe Royale, Kettner's and Pagani's were popular among the well–to–do, for French cookery and the newly fashionable claret, Champagne, and Burgundy. The middle classes clung to English fare, a Welsh rarebit or a stewed beef heart, with London stout and a joram of "hot something–and–water" afterwards. The Kitchen, in what is now Charing Cross Road, served alamode–beef gravy in pewter pots and strong ("fat") ale on the side. Most Londoners would have eaten standing at the bar of a tavern: a pork pie or sausage roll, a Banbury cake—with pale ale in any case—or possibly a brace of devilled marrow–bones or pettitoes (piglet's trotters) bought for a penny or two from an old woman outside. Up near Coventry Street was the best known baked–potato man in all of London, at whose "three–legged emporium . . . gleaming with block tin painted red, and brazen ornaments," one might get a steaming–hot potato, with salt, pepper, and bogus butter, for a penny.

If Potter and Smithers had been a bit more sober they might have gone to an oyster–house for shell–fish or turtle soup, real or mock. The better of many such

*[handwritten marginal note: Welsh Rarebit or Rabbit — a dish consisting of melted cheese, usually mixed with ale, milk & spices, served over toast]*

## MIDNIGHT SUPPER-ROOMS, HAYMARKET

Perhaps better known as oyster houses, these establishments were popular *après-theatre* resorts, as may be inferred from the formally attired gentleman with opera glasses at the oyster bar, where guests were supplied with hand-towels on rollers. To the rear a waiter ascends the stairs to the supper-rooms above, where gentlemen on the town entertained young actresses, members of the Corps de Ballet, and other female denizens of the Haymarket with steak and oysters served in discreetly curtained alcoves.

were Barron's, Barnes's, and Stone's, and the best was Scott's, a small, crowded, plain place, where lobsters, crabs, pickled and kippered salmon or herring, Yarmouth bloaters, and dried sprats could be had as well as oysters. At three shillings a dozen, Scott's oysters were not cheap, and they were eaten raw, standing at the bar, with cayenne pepper and malt vinegar, crusty bread and butter, and brown stout or strong bottled ale ("four–'arf" to costermongers). The oysters were likely to have been "natifs," a small, black, bitter mollusk from English waters that also went well with Champagne or hock.

For those who wished to mingle supper with dalliance, there were the "wild houses" of the West End, such as The Blue Posts in Cork Street, where gentlemen Stags in hats and professional Does in boas lined the bar. "Punch-houses" advertised "Rooms to Let in Rear," which was understood to mean that women were for hire there. A popular house of assignation was kept in Coventry Street by "Mother" Kate Hamilton, in her youth a much–sought–after courtesan; half the male clientele came there just to hob–nob with the obese *patronne* and exchange blue–violet repartée with her and the company. Oysters, broiled bones and such–like midnight fare were available there, as well as at the relatively new "concert rooms," "assembly rooms," casinos and dance–halls scattered throughout the West End, which were doing a roaring trade in the early morning hours. The biggest of these was the Royal Alhambra Palace in Leicester Square, done in the varnished stucco that passed for "Moorish" in Victorian London. It could accommodate 3,000 pleasure seekers at dance, drink, and dalliance.

The most fashionable of the assembly rooms was the Argyle, on the site later occupied by the Trocadero; it had an upper gallery of plush–lined booths in discreet alcoves, bars, and supper facilities. Here was Phryne in her glory: the leading courtesans of the day, each surrounded by a knot of rakes—aristocrats like Sir Mulberry Hawk, and spurious men with too many teeth like Alfred Lammle—could be seen there. Cigarettes were the rage after the Crimean War, Champagne was the rage, "devilled something" was the rage, and especially a new young Lord Mutanhead or Verisopht(NN) just down from Oxbridge, tipsy and sucking the knob of his cane: then it was feeding–time among the sharks. For these were not simple Miss Smitherses and Miss Potters out for games at Vauxhall, but devoted, successful *demi–mondaines* like Clara Willoughby, Nelly Flowers, Alice Gordon, and Nell Clifford, who grandly resided in St. John's Wood or Pimlico. The Café Riche knew them too, and Mott's in Foley Street, which had a glass-domed dance floor and a reputation for its cold roast chicken and game fowl.

The great gambling clubs of the West End were also on the watch for Mutanhead and Verisopht, such as Crockford's (now the Devonshire Club) in St. James Street. Founded in 1827, Crockford's had the finest cuisine in England; the great chef Udé was succeeded by Francatelli, who later briefly became the Queen's chef—but play was the thing, vingt-et-un and écarté. It is a drunken brawl at Crockford's that leads to a duel in *Nicholas Nickleby*, not an uncommon finish to an evening at the tables in the early years of the century.

For a Mr. Hyde on the prowl for little dress-makers and shopgirls, there was John Caldwell's raucous "Soirées Dansantes" in Dean Street, Soho, and Enon

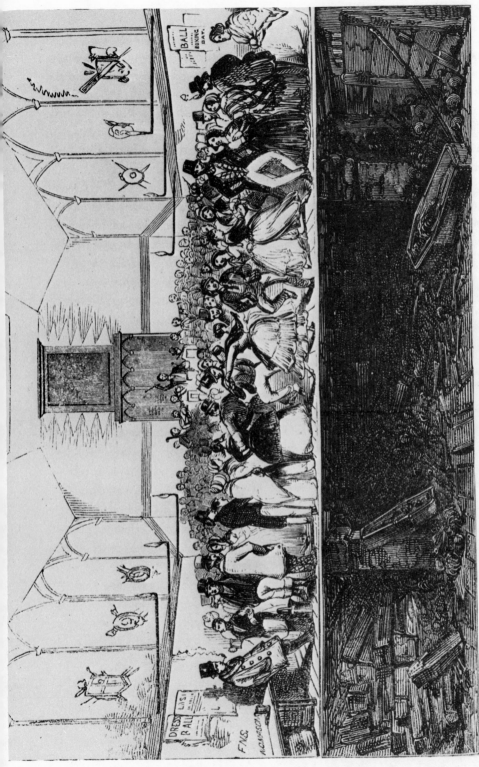

## ENON CHAPEL

Billed as the place to "Dance on the Dead—Threepence," Enon Chapel Cemetery and Dancing Salon was a notorious dance hall catering to cockney clerks and shop-assistants, whose midnight taste ran to quart pots of porter and to jigs and hornpipes. A poster at left announces a forthcoming "Dress Ball" or *Bal Masqué*. Such affairs offended pious Victorians, who viewed them as occasions for drunkenness, lubricity, and violence. That they were.

Chapel, Clement's Lane, with a charnel house under its dance-floor and a signboard outside reading "Dancing on the Dead—Threepence." Here the taste ran to paste, not diamonds, and to porter, "Crown and Anchor" jigs, "flash jigs," hornpipes, and country dances. Lower still were the dens of St. Giles and Limehouse, where Dorian Gray and John Jasper come at last, to opium dreams of pleasures unobtainable even in London.

But as for us, the night has flown, the early English dawn is breaking, and it is time for breakfast—or at least a cup of coffee at an omnibus stand in Covent Garden market—before we make our way home. Dickens, who was a great rambler and observer of the London streets at all hours, might well have done the same.

Chapter Two

# *Christmas*

*"I likes a drop of something when it's good."*
THE FAT BOY

"The paths were hard; the grass was crisp and frosty; the air had a fine, dry, bracing coldness; and the rapid approach of the grey twilight . . . made [the Pickwickians] look forward with pleasant anticipation to the comforts which awaited them. . . ."

The comforts of Christmas at the Manor Farm in Dingley Dell, Kent, are worth anticipation: warmth, laughter, games, dancing, stories, not to mention food and drink. The mood is so energetically liquid, in fact, that it prompted humorist Stephen Leacock a hundred years later to imagine what a nightmare Prohibition would have been to Mr. Pickwick's world (*The Dry Pickwick*, 1932). He shows us jolly Wardle chap–fallen, the Fat Boy thin, the wine and spirits dreadful home–made stuff, and the Christmas spirit itself grown stale. Altogether a woeful contrast to the bright scene as Dickens wrote it in 1836, jauntily epitomized for us here by Mr. Leacock:

Here is the rubicund and jovial Mr. Pickwick, together with his inimitable and immortal friends [Snodgrass, Winkle, Tupman, and his man–servant, Sam Weller] setting out by coach to visit Dingley Dell. We recall the starting of the coach from the inn–yard, the vast hampers with mysterious bottles clinking within them; the cracking of the whips of the merry postillions; the pauses by the way for a change of horses at the wayside inns where Mr. Pickwick and his friends descend from their perch to visit the bar. Here a rosy landlord behind the long mahogany dispenses sundry smoking punches and hot drinks redolent of gin and lemons. We recall the arrival at

Dingley Dell with jolly old Wardle merrily greeting his friends; more punches: festivities within doors and festivities without; hot toddies, hot negus, sugar, lemons and spices—the very atmosphere of the West Indies wafted on the Christmas air of England; skating on the ice; whist, cards and round games in the drawing-room; huge dinners and substantial suppers, the consumption of oysters by the barrel . . . and through it all the soft aroma of hot punch, mulled ale, warmed claret and smoking gin-and-lemons till . . . Mr. Pickwick and his friends sink into innocent slumber having broken enough laws—if the scene were in America [during Prohibition]—to have sent them all to the penitentiary for life.

Far from exaggerating, Leacock omits several important beverages and drinking-scenes: Pickwick treating the coach-guard to hot brandy-and-water and fumbling with cold fingers to find sixpence to pay for his coach-stop glass of ale; Sam Weller and the Fat Boy having a drop of something good together at the Blue Lion in Muggleton; the poor relations vanishing beneath the wedding breakfast-table from too much toasting in wine; Bob Sawyer and Ben Allen having brandy, oysters, and cigars in the kitchen on Christmas morning; and the utter anomaly of love-smitten Winkle and Snodgrass refusing ale and brandy all the way back to London. Nor does he identify the shrub (or "Flesh-and-Blood") taken as the Manor Farm night-cap:

> Long after the ladies had retired did the hot elder wine, well-qualified with brandy and spice, go round, and round, and round again; and sound was the sleep, and pleasant were the dreams that followed.

The use of elder wine to promote sound sleep and well-being generally was a common country practice, for the ailments that the elder (*Sambucus nigra*) could not cure might have been listed on a grain of salt. (In their "retirement," the ladies probably had a little nip of sweet wine, too.)

Then there was the ball, held the night before Christmas Eve:

> The best sitting-room at Manor Farm was a good, long, dark-panelled room with a high chimney-piece, and a capacious chimney, up which you could have driven one of the new patent cabs, wheels and all. At the upper end of the room, seated in a shady bower of holly and evergreens, were the two best fiddlers, and the only harp, in all Muggleton. In all sorts of recesses, and on all kinds of brackets, stood massive old silver candlesticks with four branches each. The carpet was up, the candles burnt bright, the

fire blazed and crackled on the hearth, and merry voices and light–hearted laughter rang through the room. If any of the old English yeomen had turned into fairies when they died, it was just the place in which they would have held their revels.

Mr. Pickwick in silk stockings ("And why not, sir—why not?") takes the head of the dance with old Mrs. Wardle—"Never was such going!" Then there is supper with a good long sitting afterwards, during which Mr. Pickwick invites forty–five people to come to London to dine with him, and rightly supposes on this account, next morning, that he may have taken something besides exercise the night before.

And finally there is Christmas Eve itself, the high point of the old festivities. The whole family and all the servants assemble in the kitchen "according to annual custom . . . observed by Wardle's forefathers from time immemorial."

> When they were all tired of blind–man's buff, there was a great game at snap–dragon, and when fingers enough were burned with that, and all the raisins were gone, they sat down by the huge fire of blazing logs to a substantial supper, and a mighty bowl of wassail, something smaller than an ordinary wash–house copper, in which the hot apples were hissing and bubbling. . . .
>
> "This," said Mr. Pickwick, looking round him, "this is, indeed, comfort."

In Dickens' time there were still farmers in outlying areas who saluted their apple–trees on Christmas Eve with a libation of cider and sops of toast. The name for this ancient fertility rite was "wassailing the apple trees," from the Anglo-Saxon *waes hael*, "be thou hale." For human consumption, ale might be substituted for cider. The name for the ingredients of Wassail, or "Lamb's Wool," probably derived from the creamy froth which forms on heated ale. Long after Wassail itself had been dolled up with wine, cake and other sophistications, a drink called "Lamb's Wool" was still made, of hot ale, toast, spices and roasted crab-apples. For Dickens, Wassail was a flexible term, as we see in the tale called "The Seven Poor Travellers":

> I had up the materials (which, together with their proportions and combinations, I must decline to impart . . .), and made a glorious jorum. Not in a bowl; for a bowl anywhere but on a shelf is a low superstition, fraught with

## CHRISTMAS EVE AT DINGLEY DELL

Mr. Wardle's family and guests join the servants around a roaring fire in the kitchen for dances, games, innocent dalliance, and "modest quenchers" of hot spiced elderberry wine in the good old-fashioned country manner, when differences of class and station were laid aside for an occasion celebrating our common humanity. Hams and woven strands of onions hang from the rafters, which for the festive season have been strung with wreaths of holly and ivy and a great armload of mistletoe.

cooling and slopping; but in a brown earthenware pitcher, tenderly suffo-
cated, when full, with a coarse cloth. It being now upon the stroke of nine, I
set out for Watts's Charity, carrying my brown beauty in my arms. . . .
there are strings in the human heart which must never be sounded by
another, and drinks that I make myself are those strings in mine.

The visitor lets a little of his secret recipe out, though, in describing "the
odours as of ripe vineyards, spice forests, and orange groves . . ." that diffuse
from the Wassail when it is deposited in a red nook of the fire.

Dickens is apparently thinking of something made with wine, spices and
roasted oranges, a beverage usually called "Bishop." We thus may drink what
we like on Christmas Eve and call it Wassail, for he always advocated following
the spirit, not the letter, of the old customs, although a narrow antiquarian
would have insisted on using a bowl made of maple wood:

> Wassail! wassail! all over the town,
> Our toast it is white and our ale it is brown,
> Our bowl is made of maplin tree:
> We be good fellows all—I drink to thee.

But Dickens' bartending experience led him to choose pitchers or jugs for his
punches and hot wine drinks. The expensive and self–conscious "boar's–head"
antiquarianism about Christmas that Disraeli and his "Young England"
movement liked did not appeal much to Dickens.

The telling of tales appealed to him enormously, though, and since goblin
stories had been a prominent part of the old tradition at Christmas, he is delighted to provide one. Old Mr. Wardle tells the tale after "filling out the
wassail with no stinted hand": Gabriel Grub is "an ill–conditioned, cross-
grained, surly fellow . . . who consorted with nobody but himself, and an old
wicker bottle" containing Hollands gin. Like Washington Irving's Rip van
Winkle, from whom he is modelled, Gabriel falls asleep and is entertained
fantastically by goblins who drink liquid fire. The experience frightens Gabriel
into becoming a better man afterwards, for

> . . . if a man turn sulky and drink by himself at Christmas time, he may
> make up his mind to be not a bit better for it; let the spirits be never so good,
> or let them be even as many degrees beyond proof, as those which Gabriel
> Grub saw in the goblins' cavern.

The Dingley Dell sort of Christmas seems such a hallowed institution that it is hard to realize how near it came to disappearing completely in the England of Dickens' youth. Cursed with the sort of mentality that in America three hundred years later conceived the Eighteenth Amendment, Oliver Cromwell proscribed the celebration of Christmas in 1643. Afterwards, industrialism and the rise of the urban proletariat (and gin–drinking) erased memories of the old rural ways: as late as 1830, Christmas was just another working day in London, unless it fell on Sunday. And Sunday was observed by many members of the working class by taking several "knocks over the liver" before noon, several more with lunch and at a tavern dog-fight in the P.M., giving the wife "a settler when she growled" at night, and getting to bed "rather muzzy–tomorrow St. Monday," according to a contemporary account. In 1824, it was said, "in the metropolis, and its immediate neighborhood, Christmas observances are little encouraged by the higher classes, and but partially by the middle ranks, while among the lower portions of the people they frequently degenerate into de-bauchery." "The lower portions," in fact, might soonest learn that it was Christmas–time by the appearance of "Christmas Gin" placards in wine-vaults, while a Christmas song of 1838 describes a drunken riot in Covent Garden Theater, after revellers had "toddled to a lushy ken for a flash of lightning, heavy wet, and whiskey, too." Given this state of affairs it is no wonder that a strict employer like Scrooge thought it unnecessary, or even wrong, to give his clerk Christmas Day off; how could he know that Bob Crat-chit would have Charles Dickens to stage–manage his Christmas for him?

It is easy to understand, too, why Dickens chose rural Kent rather than London for the Christmas scenes in *The Pickwick Papers*. On their way out from the city to Dingley Dell, the Pickwickians "take quite enough ale and brandy to enable them to bid defiance to the frost that was binding up the earth in its iron fetters." They drank to keep out the chill, of course; but also their hearty conviviality, and the cheer which awaits them at Manor Farm, stood for Dickens in bright contrast to the frost of utilitarianism and the iron fetters of urban misery. Thus his "Pickwickedness has goodness in it," as Thomas Hood noted; for Dickens invariably recommended the Old Warmth as an antidote to the New Chill.

At Manor Farm, Christmas Day itself is rather casually observed. This changed: by mid–century, Christmas trees (introduced by Prince Albert), gifts (though these were often withheld until Boxing Day), and special church ser-vices came to mark the day. Trollope in *Orley Farm* (1862) shows us an enor-

## THE STREETS: CHRISTMAS

During much of Dickens' lifetime the Christmas holiday was marked by exuberant over-indulgence. Here some intoxicated clerks beset a Town Crier while in the background a group of street musicians provide the accompaniment to dancing revellers outside a gin-palace. Disorderly scenes such as this go some way toward explaining the miserly Scrooge's reluctance to give Bob Cratchit the day off for his quiet family celebration at home.

mous Christmas breakfast, followed by an enormous early dinner, followed in turn by games in the nursery or drawing-room at twilight:

> "We shall be allowed candles now, I suppose." "Oh, no, by no means. Snap-dragon by candlelight! whoever heard of such a thing? It would wash all the dragon out of it and leave nothing but the snap . . . . the game . . . should be played by its own lurid light."

The "Ghost," in a long white sheet and with unpinned hair straggling, carries in a large dish full of raisins aflame with burning brandy. The children are not only to snatch the raisins from the burning dish but must brave the awful presence of the ghost, whose terrible face is illumined from below by the blue flames. There was another game, sometimes played at the Dickens' table after dinner, in which each person took turns making faces in the "lurid light" of a fiery bowl of spirits, conjuring up spirits and monsters; so Pip in *Great Expectations* creates the apparition of Molly Magwitch.

Then came "charades at five, with wine and sweet cake at half-past six," and later a supper, perhaps fried pudding as one Trollope figure gloomily forecasts, or bread, ale, and cold beef or turkey.

> Is not additional eating an Englishman's ordinary idea of Christmas-day?
> . . . [T]he ceremony . . . is perpetuated by butchers and beersellers, with a helping hand from the grocers. It is essentially a material festival . . . grievously overdone.

Dickens disagreed. Christmas—or indeed any sort of conviviality—was for him no mere surfeit, but a specific for physical deprivation and spiritual thirst. For no matter how much cheer there may be indoors, the shadows in Dickens cluster outside the candle-light, and the chill night presses against the window-panes. Mr. Pickwick goes to court after Christmas, thence to Fleet prison.

The famous Christmas dinner at Bob Cratchit's is such a scene. The Cratchits live in near-poverty, and their crippled child, Tiny Tim, may be spending his last Christmas on earth. No wonder that Bob and his wife somehow manage a goose ("there never was such a goose") and a pudding "like a speckled cannon-ball, so hard and firm, blazing in half of half-a-quartern of ignited brandy." Bob makes gin-punch, which he stirs round and round, and puts on the hob to simmer. After dinner, when the cloth is cleared, the hearth swept where the cooking was done, and the fire made up, the mixture is tasted and considered perfection. Apples and oranges are put on the table and a shovelful of chestnuts on the fire.

> Then all the Cratchit family drew round the hearth . . . [while] at Bob Cratchit's elbow stood the family display of glass. Two tumblers and a custard cup without a handle.
> These held the hot stuff from the jug, however, as well as golden goblets would have done; and Bob served it out with beaming looks, while the chestnuts on the fire sputtered and cracked noisily.

Against Mrs. Cratchit's protests, and in honor of The Day, they drink a generous toast to Mr. Scrooge, whom Bob calls "The Founder of the Feast"—al-

## CHRISTMAS DINNER

Although Dickens' stories did much to invest Christmas with its popular emotional content, they were part of a general resurgence of nostalgia for the traditional observance of the holidays, with its ritual exchange of tokens of affection. Here a family gathers at Christmas dinner, toasts are proposed, people take wine together, the holly-sprigged plum pudding is cut, and a hamper of wine and a decanter of brandy await later use.

though how the Cratchits manage any feast at all on Scrooge's few shillings is hard to imagine.

Scrooge himself, a miserly, cold, selfish man, has quite a different Christmas, for he is taken in hand by the Spirits of Christmas and shown a variety of affecting scenes from the past, present and future. Perhaps the most memorable of these is Fezziwig's Ball, in the counting–house where Scrooge had served his apprenticeship: there is a fiddler "tuning like fifty stomach–aches" and plunging his hot face into a pot of porter during pauses in the dancing; games and cake, and Negus and roast beef, and mince pies and plenty of beer; above all, there are people "who *would* dance, and had no notion of walking."

Scrooge is also shown the Spirit of Christmas Present, a jolly giant seated on a throne of

> turkeys, geese, game, poultry, brawn, great joints of meat, sucking–pigs, long wreaths of sausages, mince–pies, plum–puddings, barrels of oysters, red–hot chestnuts, cherry–cheeked apples, juicy oranges, luscious pears, immense twelfth–cakes, and seething bowls of punch, that made the chamber dim with their delicious steam.

These visions do not arise, as one might think, because Scrooge took a drop too much, for all he has before bed on Christmas Eve is thin gruel. When he wakes up on Christmas morning, however, he is a changed man, and hastens to make amends to his clerk, saying that they will discuss his affairs "this very afternoon, over a Christmas bowl of smoking bishop." This is surely not the least of the ways in which Dickens assures us that Scrooge is "really" changed—for when a man leaves off thin gruel, and takes to drinking hot Port (with oranges and spices in it) almost anything may happen. Bishop was a show-piece of conviviality, with its roasted Seville oranges studded with cloves. Probably introduced by Dutch sailors in the Middle Ages, it was sometimes served at guild and university banquets in cut-glass bowls resembling a bishop's mitre. Ruby Port was the wine used, but there was also a set of ecclesiastical variations, Pope, Cardinal, Archbishop, even Beadle, Churchwarden and Chorister, each with a different wine.

Boz's later Christmas stories were, as Edward Dowden complained, prone to become "bacchanalia of benevolence." But in *Great Expectations* Dickens held a rein on nostalgia. Although the Christmas chapter deals with events that happen to Pip when he is a child, odd seeds are planted in it that must be harvested long afterwards by a mature and rueful Pip. It is Christmas Eve when

## NEW YEAR'S EVE

Convivial clubs of unattached young men, like Pip's "Finches of the Grove" and Dick Swiveller's "Glorious Apollers," who liked to "make a night of it" over a reeking joram of punch, cigars of a "peculiar mildness," churchwardens, and singing, did not need Christmas or New Year's Eve to provide an excuse for revelry; but neither did they miss such occasions, either.

Pip encounters the convict Magwitch hiding in the Kentish marshes. Before dawn on Christmas Day Pip secretly takes him stolen brandy and food, and watches the convict making his Christmas meal like a hunted animal, shivering so violently that it is "quite as much as he can do to keep the neck of the bottle between his teeth without biting it off."

Later in the day there is company at the forge where Pip lives with his sister, Mrs. Gargery, and her husband, the blacksmith Joe. Uncle Pumblechook presents himself to Mrs. Gargery carrying two bottles like dumb–bells with his usual self–gratifying Christmas sentiment: " 'I have brought you, mum, a bottle of sherry wine—and I have brought you, mum, a bottle of port wine.' " It is Pumblechook who discovers that the stone bottle of brandy has been replenished with tar-water, the household emetic. Pip, the author of this sacrilege, is stricken with guilt and fear; but Mrs. Gargery busies herself "in getting the gin, the hot water, the sugar, and the lemon–peel, and mixing them"; and soon Mr. Pumblechook begins to beam, "under the influence of gin–and–water." Now there are soldiers at the door inquiring about escaped convicts and

> The interest of the impending pursuit not only absorbed the general attention, but even made my sister liberal. She drew a pitcher of beer from the cask, for the soldiers, and invited the sergeant to take a glass of brandy. But Mr. Pumblechook said sharply, "Give him wine, mum. I'll engage there's no Tar in that!"

The sergeant takes wine and rewards Pumblechook with a flattering toast:

> "With you. Hob and hob . . . The top of mine to the foot of yours—the foot of yours to the top of mine—Ring once, ring twice—the best tune on the Musical Glasses! Your health. May you live a thousand years, and never be a worse judge of the right sort than you are at the present moment of your life!"
>
> The sergeant tossed off his glass again and seemed quite ready for another glass. I noticed that Mr. Pumblechook in his hospitality appeared to forget that he had made a present of the wine, but took the bottle from Mrs. Joe and had all the credit of handing it about in a gush of joviality. Even I got some. And he was so very free of the wine that he even called for the other bottle, and handed that about with the same liberality, when the first was gone.

By having also given away food and drink that were not his to give, "innocent"

Pip is linked to the petty selfishness of Pumblechook—and a guilty chain is thus forged between their actions and Social Evil itself, as embodied in the convict Magwitch. Pip will gain a soiled fortune from Magwitch as a result, will become a "gentleman" whose origins are deep in the mire. This Christmas chapter, with all its eating and drinking, seems convivial on the surface, but it reverberates with consequence and character.

No other writer put food and drink to such good purpose—at least not so frequently—even if it be only stage–business with bottles and glasses, spirits, sugar and lemons, sipping and pledging healths, and talking more freely. But Dickens was also able to tell his Victorian readers (who knew the signals) much in this way that added to their enjoyment and understanding. Some of the old drinks, indeed, must have seemed forever tied to Dickens: a bottle of Port and a bottle of Sherry at Christmas dinner immediately put Uncle Pumblechook's

TWELFTH NIGHT

Twelfth Night closed out the holiday season with yet another party uniting family and friends, old and young, in a convivial celebration that combined a Twelfth Cake, with various prizes baked inside it, lots of hot mulled wine, Negus, and punch, and a drawing of cards to designate the reigning couple and the subordinate personages of the occasion.

legs under the table, while Wassail still calls up those jovial spirits, Wardle and the hard-headed gentleman. Gin–punch should always have the savor of Bob Cratchit's, even though a ghost of tar–water may hover over one's brandy. Other drinks in turn may have this associativeness, this richer bouquet and flavor—such at least is the aim of the chapters to follow.

# ℰ Recipes

**Wassail**

*3 pts. brown ale (or 2 pts. pale ale and 1 pt. stout); 1/2 lb. white sugar; 1 tsp. mixed spices (cinnamon or allspice, nutmeg, and mace); 6 cloves; 7 roasted crabs (or sour apples); 1 pt. hard cider; 3 lemon slices.*

Put the beer, cider, sugar, and cloves into a large enamelled pan and stir at the stove until the sugar dissolves and the mixture is quite hot. Have the roasted apples (35 minutes at 400°) ready, laid in the bottom of the serving bowl and dusted with the spices. Pour in the hot mixture, float the lemon rings, and decorate the bowl with holly sprigs. Serve.

The roasted crabapples may be peeled, cored, and mashed before being added to the bowl.

*Brown Betty* substitutes toast (on which the spices are put) for the apples and brown sugar for white. In addition, brandy at the ratio of one part to four of ale is required, together with a quartered lemon.

**Jesus College, Oxford, Wassail**
*(served on the feast of St. David)*

*1/2 lb. brown sugar; 6 pts. dark beer; 4 wineglasses Sherry; grated nutmeg; grated ginger; lemon slices.*

Dissolve sugar in a pint of heated beer and add grated nutmeg and ginger to taste. Then add Sherry and remaining beer. Heat but do not boil. Pour out to serve in an earthenware pitcher or a Wassail bowl. Float lemon slices.

**Lamb's Wool I**

*1 qt. dark beer or old ale; 4 oz. brown sugar; 1 inch stick cinnamon; 6 cloves; 2 eggs; grated ginger to taste.*

Heat the beer, sugar, and spices together. Beat eggs well in a basin. When the sugar has dissolved and the beer is hot, not boiling, pour it into an earthenware jug, and from the jug rapidly into the basin of eggs. As quickly as possible pour back and forth until a thick froth is raised. Then serve in small rummers (drinking cups).

*Lamb's Wool II*     *1/2 doz. roasted tart apples; 4 oz. brown sugar; 1 qt. strong ale or dark beer; grated nutmeg; grated ginger.*

Pulp the roasted apples and mix with sugar, spices, and hot beer until the ingredients are thoroughly melded and the whole is quite hot, but not boiling. Serve from an earthenware pitcher or Wassail bowl, as above.

*A Note on Lamb's Wool.* Lamb's Wool was sometimes called Brasenose Ale, after the college at Oxford where it was a postprandial drink on Shrove Tuesday.

*Bishop and its Clerical Brothers*     *2 or 3 Seville or other tart oranges (such as tangeloes) each studded with a dozen cloves or so; grated nutmeg; 1/2 lb. sugar; 1 lemon; 3 bottles Ruby Port.*

Roast oranges in a 400° oven (or on the hearth) until brown. Grate only the yellow of the lemon rind. Quarter the roasted oranges and place in a large saucepan with sugar, juice of a lemon, and grated rind. Add wine and heat to simmer until the ingredients are well blended, stirring the while. Serve hot in warm mugs sprinkled with freshly ground nutmeg.

The hierarchy of Bishop's clerical colleagues was determined by the color of the wine, thus: Pope=Burgundy; Cardinal=Champagne or Rhine whine; Archbishop=claret (or less frequently Sherry or Marsala); Bishop=Ruby Port; Protestant Bishop=claret and a little rum, with lemons; Churchwarden=Grand Rousillon (with tea or ale, Champagne, ginger, and cherry brandy with a dash of Port); Chorister=white wine with beaten eggs; and Beadle=raisin and ginger wines.

Some authorities advocate cloved lemons instead of oranges. Others recommend starting with whisked eggs into which the other ingredients are mixed, so bringing Bishop closer to Lamb's Wool.

One–upsmen will seek out a cone of loaf sugar or, failing that, sugar cubes for grating the lemon rind, thus adding both ingredients at once as it was done in Dickens' day. The more daring may wish to make a spectacle out of the mixing of Lamb's Wool by pouring the jugs back and forth at some distance, thereby gaining the effect of a "Yard of Flannel" (see below).

A variant of Wassail unglamorously called Cold Swig was made from a half pound of sugar, six pints of beer, four wineglasses of Sherry, and some nutmeg and ginger. After that had stood for three hours, two or three slices of toast and lemon were added. The mixture was bottled and then drunk a few days later, when it was reputed to effervesce.

Parting Cups, variously compounded of mild ale or light beer, nutmeg, sugar, and either Sherry or lemons, were a further variant, sometimes thinned with a bottle of soda water, and employed as a send-off to departing family or friends.

Chapter Three

# *"Th' Empire of Negus"*
### MILTON

" 'I'll go burn some sack; 'tis too late to go to bed now,' " says Sir Toby Belch in *Twelfth Night*; the expression was still current when Dickens wrote *Our Mutual Friend* in 1864–5: " 'They burn sherry very well here,' said Mr. Inspector, as a piece of local intelligence. 'Perhaps you gentlemen might like a bottle.' " We might, for it is a freezing night along the river–front, and a privilege to enter the very "Cosy" of the Six Jolly Fellowship Porters, where a "mouthful of fire" has been lighted for welcome, and the burnt Sherry is being made ready by Bob the potboy:

> . . . the jug steamed forth a delicious perfume, [but] its contents had not received the last happy touch which the surpassing finish of the Six Jolly Fellowship Porters imparted on such momentous occasions. Bob carried in his left hand one of those iron models of sugar-loaf hats . . . into which he emptied the jug, and the pointed end of which he thrust deep down into the fire, so leaving it for a few moments while he disappeared and reappeared with three bright drinking glasses. Placing these on the table and bending over the fire . . . he watched the wreaths of steam, until at the special instant of projection he caught up the iron vessel and gave it one delicate twirl, causing it to send forth one gentle hiss. Then he restored the contents to the jug; held over the steam of the jug, each of the three bright glasses in succession; finally filled them all, and with a clear conscience awaited the applause of his fellow–creatures.

Such hot drinks were the latest descendants of a very old family of beverages that goes back at least to the *calidae* of the Romans: cups of hot spiced wine that by the eighteenth century went by the names of Clarry, Posset, Syllabub and Hippocras. Boswell left us a recipe for Hippocras: a jug of warm white wine such as Sherry, flavored with aromatic spices, pepper and cinnamon. Any wine

*40*

## THE BAR OF "THE SIX JOLLY FELLOWSHIP PORTERS"

This "early purl house" was presided over by the formidable Abbey Potter-
son, seen here in her snug bar "girt in by corpulent little casks, and by cordial-
bottles radiant with fictitious grapes in bunches, and by lemons in nets . . .
and by the polite beer-pulls that made low bows when customers were served."
In Dickens' day, though drinks were served at the bar, they were drunk somewhere else in the tavern, the bar itself being but a place of dispensation and
observation.

might be mulled: Mrs. Pipchin, terribly upset by the fall of the House of Dombey, takes mulled Sherry, for instance, with her sweetbread; and Little Nell in *The Old Curiosity Shop* receives hot mulled Port wine when she is ill.

The French novelist Colette mentions mulled wine flavored with cinnamon and lemon that accompanied a childhood dinner of boiled chestnuts (Dickens speaks of hot chestnuts with brown Sherry), but nutmeg was the spice commonly used in England. Nutmeg graters were so common in Victorian households that the Tetterby baby teethes on one (HM). Sometimes tin graters carried moral lessons, such as "Do as you—wold—be—done—by." " 'Do, or you'll be done brown,' " retorts one cynical Dickens figure.

Dickens' own taste for mulled wine with grated nutmeg caused problems when he traveled: in America a landlord apologized for not "fixing" it right, while in Scotland the confusion was complete:

> They speak Gaelic here, of course, and many of the common people understand very little English. . . . I rang the girl upstairs and gave elaborate directions (you know my way) for a pint of sherry to be made into boiling negus; mentioning all the ingredients one by one, and particularly nutmeg. When I had finished, seeing her obviously bewildered, I said, with great gravity, "Now, you know what you're going to order?" "Oh yes. Sure." "What?"—a pause—"Just"—another pause—"Just plenty of nutbergs!"

Negus, the drink mentioned here, was made with Port or Sherry. It turns up frequently in Dickens, who wrote so knowingly about the class that favored it, the middle. Colonel Francis Negus (d. 1732), a man–about–town and confidante of the powerful of his time, had his monument in a drink. He is said to have averted a tavern brawl between some Whig and Tory bucks by concocting on the spot a novelty composed of Port, hot water, sugar and spices. For mulled wine you heat the wine; for Negus you boil the water instead; reputation is indeed a bubble. Before he limited himself to tea (a dozen or more cups in an evening), Dr. Johnson favored Port Negus. Boswell later claimed that drinking it with the Doctor had cost him many a headache, but Boswell was always ready to earn hangovers on his own hook. (Milton's reference to "Th' empire of Negus / To his utmost Port" in *Paradise Lost* seems to suggest he was fond of the beverage as well, but he is talking about an Abyssinian king.)

Negus remained popular in England until well into the nineteenth century, although the upper classes came to disdain it to the extent that the middle–class embraced it, at their balls and card-parties. Mr. Podsnap (OMF) serves his guests in Portman Square "nutmeg . . . a fragrant article, dispersed through several glasses of colored warm water"—a weak Negus, in short. At a charity ball in Rochester in *Pickwick Papers*, "wine, negus, lights and ladies" bemuse Mr. Tupman, while at Signor Billsmethi's Dancing Academy in *Sketches by Boz*, Negus shares honors among the clerks and shop-girls with spirits-and-water and "compounds" (a British excise term for rectified and flavored spirits, but Dickens may simply mean "mixed drinks"). At Vauxhall Gardens, Boz tells us, they stretched the Negus (and the rack punch) as far as they sliced the ham thin—and *that* was a joke of very long standing indeed.

In "The Schoolboy's Story," Old Cheeseman, a poor second Latin master, suffers the persecution of the boys and the snubs of superiors until he turns up missing one day, thought to have been drowned. In fact he has come into a large fortune, at which the master fawns and the boys are in a tremble. Old Cheeseman, however, calls them all "dear companions and old friends" and treats them to a spread of "fowls, tongues, preserves, fruits, confectioneries, jellies, neguses, barley-sugar temples, trifles, crackers—eat all you can and pocket what you like—all at Old Cheeseman's expense." Nothing could be farther from this cheer than the glass of cold Negus which Colonel Newcome muses over on a sad occasion; and it is from Thackeray too that we learn that the word was pronounced "neegus." As for barley-sugar castles, one may find them gracing the banquet-tables of the mighty as depicted in Victorian engravings, with tiny flags flying over the sugary battlements.

Harold Skimpole (BH), who is said to be a caricature of the writer Leigh Hunt, takes claret and a peach and coffee for breakfast, but by evening he graduates to Negus, and this stimulates him to sing an old ballad that is still popular on the long-necked banjo circuit: "Thrown on the wide world, doom'd to wander and roam / Bereft of his parents, bereft of a home" and so on. It is a second glass of warm sherry Negus which brings out little Dr. Chillip in *David Copperfield* (" 'Quite an uncommon dissipation' "); and Negus again brings out the Reverend Mr. Stiggins when he visits Mr. Pickwick in the Fleet Prison. Since his favorite, pineapple rum, is not permitted by prison authorities, Stiggins is prevailed upon to accept a substitute: "a bottle of port wine, warmed with a little water, spice and sugar, as being grateful to the stomach, and savouring less of vanity than many other compounds." When the Negus arrives, Sam Weller says of it:

"Wot do you think o' that for a go o' wanity warm, sir?"
Mr. Stiggins made no verbal answer, but . . . tasted the contents of the

glass . . . put his umbrella on the floor, and tasted it again: passing his hand placidly across his stomach twice or thrice; he then drank the whole at a breath, and smacking his lips, held out the tumbler for more.

Nor was Mrs. Weller behindhand in doing justice to the composition. The good lady began by protesting that she couldn't touch a drop—then took a small drop—then a large drop—then a great many drops; and her feelings being . . . powerfully affected . . . she dropped a tear with every drop of negus, and so got on, melting the feelings down, until at length she arrived at a very pathetic and decent pitch of misery.

With the second jug of Negus the Rev. Stiggins is lecturing Sam upon the vice of intoxication, "and staggering to and fro in the excitement of his eloquence, is fain to catch at the back of a chair to preserve his perpendicular."

Such scenes are typical of Dickens' way of playing host to his figures and letting them "come out in their own character" over a drop or several of their favorite. There is, for a memorable example, the evening at the Maypole Inn (BR), when a mystery crucial to the novel is brewing in an upper room, giving rise to delighted speculation among the fireside denizens below:

It was felt to be such a holiday and special night that . . . every man put down his sixpence for a can of flip, which grateful beverage was brewed with all dispatch, and set down in the midst of them on the brick floor; both that it might simmer and stew before the fire, and that its fragrant steam, rising up among them, and mixing with the wreaths of vapour rising from their pipes, might shroud them in a delicious atmosphere of their own, and shut out all the world. The very furniture seemed to mellow and deepen in its tone; the ceiling and walls looked blacker and more highly polished, the curtains of a ruddier red; the fire burnt high and clear, and the crickets on the hearthstone chirped with a more than wonted satisfaction.

Here it is the old inn itself which is "brought out," for it is indeed a principal character in the novel.

Unlike Negus, Flip might be made of either ale or wine, with eggs whisked up in it. A well-appointed old hostelry such as the Maypole would have had a "flip–dog" by the fire, a short poker which was heated and plunged hissing into the expectant flip, giving it a pleasant burnt taste. Pip has Flip, in *Great Expectations*, on the eve of his departure from the forge to go to London for to be a gentleman, while Mrs. Chickenstalker in *The Chimes* orders Flip sent in to a New Year's Eve party: "Her notion of a little flip did honor to her character,

## NEGUS IN FLEET PRISON

Fleet Prison in the last century offered all the comforts of home. In this instance the Reverend Mr. Stiggins, denied his usual hot pineapple-rum-and-water-warm-with, must settle for Negus when visiting Sam Weller "on board the Fleet." The Negus, we assume, was brought over from a nearby "whistling shop." The unaccustomed beverage appears to have rather carried Mr. Stiggins away with it, to Tony Weller's infinite amusement.

for the pitcher steamed and smoked and reeked like a volcano, and the man who carried it was faint."

Dickens' own recipe for cold Flip appears in *Little Dorrit*: "the yolk of a new-laid egg, beaten up . . . with a glass of sound sherry, nutmeg and powdered sugar. . . . " He took this as a "pull-me-up" at the intermissions of his public readings. Flip can also be made with ale, and so shades into a numerous old family of hot ale drinks. At the Jolly Sandboys in *The Old Curiosity Shop* the strolling Punch-and-Judy showman, Tom Codlin, orders a pint of warm ale before dinner, whereupon

> the landlord retired to draw the beer, and presently returning with it, applied himself to warm the same in a small tin-vessel shaped funnel-wise, for the convenience of sticking it far down in the fire and getting at the bright places. This was soon done, and he handed it over to Mr. Codlin with that creamy froth upon the surface which is one of the happy circumstances attendant on mulled malt.

Bracket or Bragget, on the other hand, was ale, honey and pepper, while Rum Fustian, an "Oxford Nightcap," required ale, wine, gin, eggs, sugar and spices—everything *but* rum. There was Tewahdidle (ale, brandy, sherry, spices and sugar) and Jehu's Nectar (ale, gin-and-bitters and ginger, heated and "drunk frothing"), at which Oxbridge wits no doubt reminded each other that the drink should be frothing too.

Egg-hot, probably made with porter, eggs, sugar, nutmeg and ginger, is prepared for David Copperfield and herself by Mrs. Micawber on an unhappy evening when Mr. Micawber languishes for debt in the King's Bench Prison. In *The Uncommercial Traveller* (1860) Dickens describes a childhood encounter with a drink called Caudle, when his nurse took him to a house where "a lady . . . had four children (I am afraid to write five, though I fully believe it was five) at a birth." The deceased infants were laid out side by side on a clean cloth, while hot Caudle was handed round to sustain the visitors. The ingredients of Caudle appear in the *Sketches*: "warm beer, spice, eggs and sugar [with] such a stirring about of little messes in tiny saucepans on the hob." Caudle usually contained crumbled toast or gruel, and was revered for its restorative powers. Peppermint Caudle was served as a stirrup-cup in Milton's time, according to Robert Graves, but nutmeg was the usual Victorian flavoring. Mrs. Gamp, the nurse in *Chuzzlewit*, says that her imaginary friend Mrs. Harris carried in her pocket "a bit o' ginger, and a grater like a blessed infant's shoe, in tin, with a little heel to put the nutmeg in: as many times I've seen and said, and used for caudle when required, within the month." Surely thinking of Mrs. Gamp, Dickens' friend Douglas Jerrold used the name "Mrs. Caudle" for a termagant matron in a series of humorous pieces that helped to spark the popularity of *Punch*.

## THE CODDLED COUPLE

In the age before aspirin, tranquilizers, and sleeping-pills, one prepared for bed with a "composing draught"—a nightcap, mulled wine, caudle, or the like—perhaps made on the hearth, as here, where much of the preparation and enjoyment of food and drink took place.

Dickens mentions "brose," a compound of Scotch, honey or brown sugar, oatmeal, and cream. Thomas Hardy's Mayor of Casterbridge gets drunk at a village fair on "Furmity," a similar concoction with wheat that was surreptitiously spiked with rum by the old woman who served it. Ale–berry (oatmeal, ale, wine, lemon juice, and spices served hot with toast) was an older version of what one lexicographer called a "sloppy mess"—which leads us to wonder if the modern pejorative sense of the word "mess" (as in messy) did not derive from its original neutral meaning, "a serving of food" (as in "a mess of pottage") by association with Caudles and Furmities.

By far the most popular of the hot ale drinks, though, was Purl. Purl began life in the Middle Ages as a mixture of wormwood, gentian, calamus, horseradish, and other bitter herbs, steeped in a quantity of ale for several months, then strained and drunk warm as a medicine. In a simpler form it was taken as "The Morning Draught" by such as Samuel Pepys, who regularly stepped over to a nearby tavern from the Admiralty to have a mid-morning breakfast, perhaps a kipper and a baked potato, and a pint of Purl. By Victorian times Purl was composed of hot ale, gin, sugar, and spices. Its matitudinal nature is duly noted in *Our Mutual Friend*, at the Six Jolly Fellowship Porters, where those aforementioned "fireside tin utensils, like models of sugar-loaf hats,"

> mulled your ale, or heated for you those delectable drinks, purl, flip, and dog's nose. The first of these humming compounds was a specialty of the Porters, which, through an inscription on its door-posts, gently appealed to your feelings as, "The Early Purl House." For, it would seem that purl must always be taken early. . . .

Early Purl is enjoyed at the Peacock by Charley in "The Holly-Tree," who testifies to its being "uncommonly good." "The Peacock" at Islington was a familiar coaching stop, where Tom Brown takes stout on his way to Rugby; and he has Purl at another inn along the way. On the Thames, bum-boatmen who catered to sailors from small barges or yawls made and sold Purl. The ale was carried in two four-gallon casks with a one-gallon cask of cheap gin, and the mixture was heated on sheet-iron stoves, then passed up in pewter pots to thirsty tars. The cry that floated over the foggy Thames was "Pint o' purl ahoy!" Ashore again, the watermen who attended to the horses of hackney coaches, "with dim lanterns in their hands and large brass plates on their breasts, retired to their watering houses [after a long night's work in the Haymarket] to solace themselves with the creature comforts of pipes and purl."

The remarkable drink called "Dog's Nose" was just a hasty purl, thrown together for the man in the street. The drink must have been nearly forgotten by 1857, when a question about it cropped up in a rigorous "exam" set for Cambridge Dickens buffs. The answer, no doubt, was in *Pickwick Papers*, when the Wellers visit a temperance meeting that is hearing reports on recent converts:

"H. Walker, tailor, wife, and two children. When in better circumstances, owns to having been in the constant habit of drinking ale and beer; says he is not certain whether he did not twice a week, for twenty years taste 'dog's nose,' which your committee find upon inquiry, to be compounded of warm porter, moist sugar, gin, and nutmeg (a groan, and 'So it is!' from an elderly female). Is now out of work and penniless; thinks it must be the porter (cheers) or the loss of the use of his right hand; is not certain which, but thinks it very likely that, if he had drunk nothing but water all his life, his fellow–workman would never have stuck a rusty needle in him, and

## DICK SWIVELLER, PURL, AND THE MARCHIONESS

Dick Swiveller, whose "rosy wine" was a swig of gin and water or a tankard of porter, here consoles his unrequited love with a pot of hot purl before going home to commune with his flute. He introduces a poor servant-girl, dubbed the Marchioness, to the pleasures of the pot, urging her for safety's sake to "moderate her transports."

thereby occasioned his accident (tremendous cheering). Has nothing but cold water to drink, and never feels thirsty (great applause)."

At low houses such as The Three Cripples in *Oliver Twist*, Purl was called "Hot Flannel" by men of the Bill Sikes stamp: hot ale, gin, sugar, nutmeg and eggs. When the eggy mixture was poured back and forth between two jugs, an adroit landlord could make "a yard of flannel" by gradually increasing the distance between the jugs, to the applause of his audience.

Purl is taken by Dick Swiveller in *The Old Curiosity Shop* as a nightcap. He knows a "particular recipe" for it that we wish he had vouchsafed us, since he "made a fragrant compound, which sent forth a grateful steam," and he sips it while playing cribbage with the Marchioness, the child-servant who has a permanent cold and doesn't know her own name or age. Dick gives her a sip too, but advises her to "moderate her transports" since she's not used to it. Apparently not so used to it himself, Dick unsteadily gets himself home, musing upon his thwarted love for one Sophie Wackles: "some men in his blighted position would have taken to drinking; but as Mr. Swiveller had taken to that before, he only took to playing the flute . . . [and] breathed into the flute the whole sentiment of the purl down to its very dregs."

"Oxford Nightcaps" of hot ale or wine were so well-known that their fame has even fallen confusedly on the ears of flighty Mrs. Nickleby, who remarks to Nicholas that " 'young men at college are uncommonly particular about their nightcaps, and . . . Oxford nightcaps are quite celebrated for their strength and goodness; so much so, indeed, that the young men never dream of going to bed without 'em. . . . ' " But whether we have here shed light upon the origin of the expression "to tie one on" we leave to the judgment of others.

**Mulled Wine**
*(An excellent French receipt)*

*1 1/2 wineglass of water; 1/4 oz. spice (24 cloves, more ginger than cinnamon); 3 oz. sugar; 1 or 2 strips orange rind (optional: if used, boil with spice); 1 pt. Port or claret.*

"Boil a wineglassful and a half of water, a quarter of an ounce of spice (cinnamon, ginger slightly bruised, and cloves), with three ounces of fine sugar, until they form a thick syrup, which must not on any account be allowed to burn. Pour in a pint of port wine, and stir it gently until it is on the point of *boiling* only: it should then be served immediately. The addition to the spices of a strip or two of orange–rind cut extremely thin, gives to this beverage the flavour of Bishop. In France light claret takes the place of port wine in making it, and the better kinds of *vin ordinaire* are very palatable thus prepared.

*Obs.* Sherry, or very fine raisin or ginger wine, prepared as above, and stirred hot to the yolks of four fresh eggs, will make good egg–wine."

MRS. ELIZA ACTON

**Ale Flip or Egg Hot**

*3 pts. ale; 1 blade mace; 1 clove; 1 tbsp. sugar; 1 egg white; 2 egg yolks; small piece of butter.*

Put into a saucepan the ale, sugar, mace, clove, and butter and bring to a simmer. Beat the egg white and yolks thoroughly, mixing them with a tablespoon of cold ale. Mix all together and then pour the whole rapidly from one jug to another to froth it well. Serve hot in tankards.

**Egg Flip**

*3 eggs; 3 oz. lump sugar; grated nutmeg; grated ginger; 1 pt. strong ale; 2 wineglasses gin or rum (preferably gin).*

Beat together the whites and yolks of eggs and sugar. Add to

1/2 pt. ale and heat to nearly boiling. Add spirit and spices and combine with 1/2 pt. hot ale in a jug. Pour back and forth between jugs until well frothed. Serve hot in tankards or pots.

### Hot Ale Cup

*4 tbsp. moist sugar; plenty of cloves and cinnamon; 2 tbsp. American bitters; 1 qt. hot ale; 2 wineglasses gin; 3 wineglasses Noyau.*

To the hot ale add gin, Noyau, bitters, spices, and sugar. Stir well to mix thoroughly and serve hot in tankards.

### Copus Cup

*1 slice toast; 1 slice lemon; 12 cloves; grated nutmeg; 2 qts. hot ale; 4 wineglasses brandy; 3 wineglasses Noyau; 1 1/2 lb. lump sugar; juice of 1 lemon.*

Heat ale and add brandy, Noyau, sugar, and lemon juice. Mix well. Stick lemon slice to toast with cloves, dust with nutmeg, and float on surface of an earthenware pitcher. Serve hot in stemmed glasses.

Leo Engel and the Davies brothers offer a number of recipes for Flip in which brandy, rum, or a combination of the two is substituted for ale, or in which gin is added to ale or porter in the ratio of one part gin to four parts ale. The latter is properly called Purl, and brings us naturally to the following:

### Rumfustian

*2 egg yolks; 1 tbsp. sugar; grated nutmeg; spice (cinnamon or allspice and mace); 1/2 pt. old ale; 1 wineglass Sherry; 1 wineglass gin; grated peel of one lemon.*

Beat in a jug the yolks of two eggs with a tbsp. of sugar. Mix separately ale, gin, Sherry, spice, and lemon rind. Let the mixture come to a simmer, then pour in the beaten eggs, whisking rapidly. Serve hot, with nutmeg grated on top, in a tankard.

*Sack Posset*
*(Sir Fleetwood Fletcher's*
*lyrical receipt)*

"From fam'd Barbadoes, on the western main,
Fetch sugar, ounces four; fetch sack from Spain
A pint; and from the Eastern Indian coast
Nutmeg, the glory of our northern toast;
O'er flaming coals let them together heat
Till the all-conquering sack dissolve the sweet;
O'er such another fire put eggs just then,
New-born from tread of cock and rump of hen;
Stir them with steady hand and conscience pricking,
To see th' untimely end of ten fine chickens:
From shining shelf take down the brazen skillet,
A quart of milk from gentle cow will fill it;
When boil'd and cold, put milk and sack to eggs,
Unite them firmly like the Triple League,
And on the fire let them together dwell
Till miss sing twice—you must not kiss and tell:
Each lad and lass take up a silver spoon,
And fall on fiercely like a starv'd dragoon."

By omitting the eggs and adding a little lemon rind, then scalding the milk until it separates into curds and whey, we can make White Wine Whey or Milk Posset. If some white peppercorns are boiled with the milk, we have a Pepper Posset, a medicinal compound once employed to promote perspiration. By adding a quart of fresh cider to a quart of milk and a gill (1/4 pt.) of Sherry, plus the grated peel of 1 lemon and sugar to taste, a Cider Posset is made.

This leads us to:

*Caudle*

*4 cups boiling water; 1/4 cup oatmeal; pinch of salt; 2 pts. ale or stout, heated; grated rind of 1 lemon; 2 tbsp. brown sugar; powdered mace; powdered ginger.*

Cook all ingredients together (except the ale) until the oatmeal is tender—about 10 minutes if quick or instant oatmeal is used. Add ale or stout and mix. Serve in tankards.

Caudle is similar to Furmity and Atholl Brose, but the latter is made with Scotch whisky and brown sugar or Drambuie alone.

*Port Wine Negus*    *1 pt. Port; 1/4 lb. lump sugar; grated rind and juice of*
*1 lemon; 1 qt. boiling water; grated nutmeg to taste*

Grate the lemon rind on the lump sugar into a jug of Port, then add the juice of the lemon, strained. Pour in the boiling water and dust with nutmeg. Stopper the jug with a clean napkin or cloth until the mixture cools. Serve.

Sherry Negus is made with an extra quarter-pound of sugar, and a wineglassful of Noyau or Maraschino may be added.

*Purl*    Purl is made with porter sweetened with sugar, given character with spices, and strengthened with gin. Porter may be approximated, when not available, with dark beer or with two parts of sound English or Canadian ale and one part of stout. Heat this with a little grated ginger and sugar and serve out into mugs, adding a shot of gin and a dusting of nutmeg.

*A Note on Drinking Vessels.* Drinks made with eggs are not pretty, so they are best served in pewter or earthenware tankards or pots. Clear hot drinks were commonly served by our grandsires in stemmed glasses to protect the fingers.

*A Caveat.* The drinks above in which milk is a constituent were originally made with whole milk, unpasteurized and with the cream still in it. Modern tipplers will find that these recipes will produce better results if an attempt is made to reconstitute whole milk from the fragments in which it is now purveyed.

Chapter Four

# *Pickwick, Principle, and Punch*

In the days of Dickens' young manhood, a great bowl of punch was still the hub of an evening's festivity. At least one Regency buck was depicted in his club portrait mixing a bowl of punch, and for a woman trying to stay afloat in what was very much a man's world, like Becky Sharp in Thackeray's *Vanity Fair*, the ability to make good punch was an indispensable skill. A familiar convivial scene in those days was the candle–lit private dining room of a good inn, the fire ruddling the faces of a dozen or so gentlemen who have finished dining, finished their Port (which has ruddled their faces too), and are now gathered about a table on which stands a huge china bowl, empty as yet, but surrounded promisingly by sundry bottles, lemons, oranges, a sharp paring knife, a big spoon for stirring. There is moist sugar that will dissolve readily in the mixture, and also a pyramid of loaf sugar, on which the lemons will be rubbed to bring out their essential oil. (An order of punch might even appear on a landlord's bill as "A rub of punch.")

Now a steaming kettle is brought in, and the Compounder is led forward: a gentleman of proven experience, able to keep his own counsel in the midst of roaring conviviality. If Dickens were in the company, he was usually the man. The Compounder pours and mixes, tastes and considers, and at length is satisfied; brushfire conversations sputter out, and in the echoes of a ringing toast the first glassfuls are drunk off. It is as if the spirits were poured upon redhot embers, for talk and laughter burst out louder than before; the punch is praised and appraised, and suggestions are made to the Compounder, who receives them with courteous gravity but remains tranquil in his view that the punch is well enough as it is. After the first few rounds nobody cares anyway, and some gentlemen pour spirits-and-water directly into their glasses, relying on a residuum of sugar and lemon as a Solomon's Stone. There were always some who agreed with the elderly Irish churchman who thought adding water to punch was "just a cruel spoilin' " of it; he added the spirits to the water instead,

*55*

## DICKENS TAKES PUNCH WITH SOME OF HIS CHARACTERS

Left to right: Mr. Pickwick, Tony Weller, Signor Mantalini, Sam Weller, Mr. Micawber,
Dickens, Sarah Gamp, Rev. Stiggins, Bumble the Beadle, and Mr. Pecksniff.

whereby "ivrey dhrop ye put in is afther makin' the punch bether and
bether."

The famous party at Bob Sawyer's lodgings in Lant Street (PWP) is of this
kind. Bob has bought spirits at a wine–vaults in the Borough High Street
(where Dickens may have bought them himself, since he lived for a short time
in Lant Street) and has carefully seen them home; he has made punch in a bed
pan in his bedroom, borrowed glasses from a public-house—but he has ne-
glected to pay his rent. Three hours of cards and punch from a white jug are
preliminary to supper (underdone beef and ham, unopenable oysters, strong
cheese, and porter in a can), following which more punch is set on the table,
with cigars and brandy. Bob only had four glasses to begin with, his landlady's
"little thin blown–glass tumblers," while those borrowed from the public-house
are "great dropsical, bloated articles, each supported on a huge gouty leg," and

Mrs. Raddles' girl has taken them all away to be washed. Bob is afraid the whole lot will be confiscated, and is enormously relieved when they come back, but his equanimity is brief: " 'You can't have no warm water. . . . Missis Raddle raked out the kitchen fire afore she went to bed, and locked up the kittle.' "

Bob's "heart–sickening attempts to rally" under this blow cause the company (the Pickwickians and several of Bob's medical–student friends) to attach itself with "extra cordiality to cold brandy–and–water." This in turn leads to a rousing argument between Mr. Noddy and Mr. Gunter ("the gentleman in the shirt" decorated with anchors, which are Temperance symbols of the Band of Hope, and also the trademark of the close–by Barclay & Perkins brewery), after which Jack Hopkins sings a song to a mixture of two tunes, while everyone else sings it to the tune he knows best, so that "the effect is very striking indeed." Indeed it strikes the ear of Mrs. Raddle, who scolds the party to a premature end, rattling the unoffending Mr. Pickwick downstairs with " 'Get along with you, you old wretch! . . . You're worse than any of 'em.' " The Pickwickians hurry away, with Ben Allen for company, as far as London Bridge, but there he is overcome by the varied emotions of the evening (and by punch, porter, and cold brandy–and–water), bursts into tears, knocks his hat over his eyes, and "making the best of his way back . . . knocked double knocks at the door of the Borough Market office, and took short naps on the steps alternately, until daybreak, under the firm impression that he lived there and has forgotten the key."

This is a Man's World unabashed, but with the great bowl at its center, the Female Principle, Source and Symbol of (masculine convivial) Life. The toasts and songs rise in vigor if not in virtue; candles are pulled from their sockets to light pipes and cigars, and also to serve as batons for the singers, who anoint themselves liberally with wax and spend the next morning moodily picking at it in their offices, chambers and vestries. Horses, dogs, shooting-boxes, footmen, and mistresses are extolled or found wanting; friendships fester or bloom, bets are made and duly recorded, in the manner shown in *Pickwick*:

> "I see there's a notice up this morning about Boffer," observed Mr. Simmery. "Poor devil, he's expelled the house!"
>
> "I'll bet you ten guineas to five, he cuts his throat," said Wilkins Flasher, Esquire.
>
> "Done," replied Mr. Simmery.
>
> "Stop! I bar," said Wilkins Flasher, Esquire, thoughtfully. "Perhaps he may hang himself."

## AN APOTHECARY'S PUNCH

Beakers, a funnel, and a mortar and pestle are pressed into service for a punch party for Bob Sawyer, Pickwick, and Winkle. The cigars could be "toofahs," after "two for" whatever the going rate was. Alcohol was so much a part of the Victorian pharmacopoeia that a sick man was hard put to decide between the apothecary and the publican for treatment.

"Very good," rejoined Mr. Simmery, pulling out the gold pencil-case again. "I've no objection to take you that way. Say, makes away with himself."

"Kills himself, in fact," said Wilkins Flasher, Esquire.

"Just so," replied Mr. Simmery, putting it down. 'Flasher—ten guineas
to five, Boffer kills himself.' "

How much did Dickens participate in this sort of thing? We know that some
of Dickens' best friends were given at times to excess: George Cruikshank
before he took the pledge, Wilkie Collins, Augustus Egg, G.A. Sala, Leigh
Hunt. If Dickens had any criticism of their behavior he kept it to himself; and
he liked to be thought of as their companion in "diablerie," as a respite from
bouts of work. He objected to Cruikshank's Teetotalism, and chaffed John
Forster for not drinking spirits. His invitations to friends were often specific:
"Scotch whisky and cigars," "*Extraordinary* (underlined four times) French
brandy"—surely smuggled. "We have been in the house two hours," wrote
Dickens invitingly to Thomas Beard from his summer place at Broadstairs,
"and the dining-parlour closet already displays a good array of bottles, duly
arranged by the writer hereof—the spirits labelled 'Gin,' 'Brandy,' 'Hollands,'
in autograph character—and the wine tasted and approved."

Abstaining from porter on doctor's orders he vowed was hard on him—"I
done it though" (by switching to Hollands gin). He enjoyed talking to bartenders, and probably sampled most potions then current. He took Sherry and
Champagne backstage to help him through his frenzied theatrical activities,
when he was sometimes both stage-manager and leading actor; and he sometimes drank wine while he wrote, probably very sparingly. Frequent travelling
gave him a wide experience of wayside ale–houses, such as the delightful "Peal
of Bells" in "Tom Tiddler's Ground," inns, hotels, and private hospitality. He
and his wife (who wrote a cookbook under the name of Lady Maria Clutter-
buck) set a lavish table at home, with the best wines, ales, and spirits. "Will you
tell me where that Punch is to be bought, what one has to ask for, and what the
cost is. It has made me very uneasy in my mind," wrote Dickens to Harrison
Ainsworth; and from another letter, "Have you tried the punch yet; if yes, did
it succeed? if not, why not?"

Drink as well as food came readily to his mind as he wrote; hundreds of
scenes involve drinking, often as background, but sometimes as the principal
"business." We learn a great deal about Mr. Pecksniff, for instance, while
Martin Chuzzlewit and his friends are discussing whether they want to toast
him or not; which, as each of them does it in his own way, tells us something
about them as well. Food and drink are often enough used as figures of speech;
Miss Miggs' expression on one occasion mingles many emotions "in a kind of
physiognomical punch" (BR). *Hard Times* opens with a picture of Mr. Grad-

grind visiting his model utilitarian school: the room is "a vault"; Gradgrind's eyes are set in "commodious cellarage" under his brow; his bald pate is "the crust of a plum–pie," and the children are like "vessels . . . ready to have imperial gallons poured into them until they were full to the brim." Neither *Hard Times* nor *Chuzzlewit* is in any sense a "convivial" novel.

It was commonly agreed by those who knew him best that Dickens "liked to dilate in imagination over the brewing of a bowl of punch. . . . It was the sentiment of the thing and not the thing itself that engaged his attention." He liked the "paraphernalia of good cheer," as another American friend said. But he was cautious about excess, for it interfered with his real intoxication, work.

But the brewing of punch in company was great theater, and it became an important part of Dickens' rather theatrical sociability. "Into assemblies of dimmer personalities he blazed like a star making an entrance," Edgar and Eleanor Johnson remark. He often wrapped himself in a blue cloak with velvet facings, a blue dress–coat with brass buttons and an embroidered shirt–bosom. "Gleaming patent leather encased his feet, primrose–yellow gloves his hands. His waistcoats were sensational—green and crimson velvet, black satin embroidered with flowers, broad stripes of blue and purple." His hair was touched up with brilliantine, and he glittered with "gold rings, jeweled tie–pins, watch chains, and fobs."

Dickens' punch–making, Hesketh Pearson imagines, was a ritualistic performance, accompanied by serious comments on the ingredients, humorous asides about the effect they would have upon the different drinkers, elaborate speeches on the concoction, and when the business was completed to his satisfaction, the brewage was poured out in the manner of a conjuror producing strange articles from a hat.

The original of the many Dickens figures who could turn the least occasion into a celebration by brewing lemon punch was the novelist's father. John Dickens is especially evident in the character of Wilkins Micawber, whom David Copperfield found on one occasion in his usual state of insolvency and gloom, and

> . . . to divert his thoughts from this melancholy subject . . . led him to the lemons. His recent despondency . . . was gone in a moment. I never saw a man enjoy himself amid the fragrance of lemon–peel and sugar, the odour of burning rum, and the steam of boiling water, as Mr. Micawber did that afternoon. It was wonderful to see his face shining at us out of a thin cloud of these delicate fumes, as he stirred, and mixed, and tasted, and

looked as if he were making, instead of punch, a fortune for his family down to the latest posterity.

Punch-making in the midst of adversity becomes such a recognizable leit motif of Micawber that when he must expose that "transcendent and immortal hypocrite and perjuror," Uriah Heep, David is startled to see his friend

putting the lemon–peel into the kettle, the sugar into the snuffer–tray, the spirit into the empty jug, and confidently attempting to pour boiling water

## MICAWBER PRESIDES OVER THE PUNCH

Entertaining David Copperfield and Traddles whilst hiding out from his creditors, Wilkins Micawber brews punch at the family hearth, employing a pitcher from the wash-stand to hold the ambrosial nectar. Austere punch-makers like Dickens scorned the silver punch bowl as an affectation, preferring instead an earthenware jug warming on the hearth, the mouth stuffed with a large napkin.

out of a candlestick. . . . He clattered all his means and implements to-gether, rose from his chair, pulled out his pocket–handkerchief, and burst into tears.

"My dear Copperfield," said Mr. Micawber, behind his handkerchief, "this is an occupation, of all others, requiring an untroubled mind, and self–respect. I cannot perform it. It is out of the question."

Following his declaration, however, with mind and heart now clear and mindful of his determination to make a new life in Australia with his family, he is once again able to make punch,

peeling the lemons with his own clasp–knife, which, as became the knife of a practical settler, was about a foot long; and which he wiped, not wholly without ostentation, on the sleeve of his coat. . . . In a similar anticipa-tion of life . . . in the Bush, Mr. Micawber . . . served it out . . . in a series of villainous little tin pots; and I never saw him enjoy anything so much as drinking out of his own particular pint pot, and putting it in his pocket at the close of the evening.

The Kenwigs family of *Nickleby* are always in adversity, like the Micawbers and the senior Dickenses, but still manage to find the materials for a bowl of convivial punch for their "bohemian" guests, while in the same novel Mr. Crummles' theatricality is manifestly that of John Dickens:

Mr. Crummles, who knew full well that he should be the subject of the forthcoming toast, sat gracefully in his chair, with his arm thrown over the back, and now and then lifted his glass to his mouth and drank a little punch, with the same air with which he was accustomed to take long draughts of nothing, out of the pasteboard goblets in banquet scenes.

The basic chemistry of punch was outlined for Victorians in a little verse:

> Whene'er a bowl of punch we make,
> Four striking opposites we take—
> The strong, the small, the sharp, the sweet,
> Together mixed most kindly meet.

Or: spirits, water or tea, lemons, and sugar, with wine and other "softeners" and flavorings. The classic proportions were "one sour, two sweet, three strong and four weak." All the usual spirits, and arrack, were used in punches. Rum punch was very popular; it is made by lawyer Sampson Brass in *The Old Curiosity Shop* with Jamaica rum from Quilp's private stock, and "hot water, fragrant lemons, white lump sugar, and all things fitting." Among the latter was usually Angostura Bitters, unboiled water to make a "creamy head," powdered sugar for the same purpose, or "capillaire" instead of sugar; and a great deal of undivided attention was given to the peeling of the lemons.

"The juice and thin peel of a Seville orange add variety of flavour, especially to Whisky Punch; lime juice is also excellent. . . . Several additions may be made to *soften* the flavour of Punch; as a wineglass of Port, or of Sherry; a tablespoon of red currant jelly; a piece of fresh butter . . . or half Rum and half Shrub. . . . Tamarinds will give Punch a flavour closely resembling Arrack. A tablespoonful of Guava jelly much improves Punch." Such were the *Hints for the Table*, offered in 1860. Walter Gay in *Dombey and Son* promises to bring back limes for Captain Cuttle's punch from Barbados, along with "turtles" for his soup and "preserves," probably guava.

*Pickwick Papers* is very like punch itself, a happy blend of "strong and small, sharp and sweet." Or better, it is a convivial gathering brought together and kept going by a master host. It is also, as someone has said, a nearly complete *vade mecum* of late–Georgian and early–Victorian drinking: drink is mentioned about two hundred and fifty times, only the last reference being to abstinence. There are 35 breakfasts, 32 dinners, 10 luncheons, 10 teas and 8 suppers. Pickwick's man–servant, Sam Weller, likes to cry "Pickwick and Principle," but he might as well cry "Punch and Pickwick." It is cold punch, for instance, which undoes Mr. Pickwick when he joins old Wardle's hunting–party in the Kentish countryside. They stop for lunch under a large oak, where the Fat Boy unlimbers two stone bottles, one of beer, the other of cold punch—gin punch, no doubt, since it is warm weather:

> "Good," said Mr. Pickwick, smacking his lips. "Very good. I'll take another. Cool; very cool. Come, gentlemen," continued Mr. Pickwick, still retaining his hold upon the jar, "a toast. Our friends at Dingley Dell."

Then Mr. Pickwick looks earnestly at the stone bottle, saying,

> "Well, that certainly is most capital cold punch . . . and the day is extremely warm, and—Tupman, my dear friend, a glass of punch?"
>
> "With the greatest delight," replied Mr. Tupman; and having drank that glass, Mr. Pickwick took another, just to see whether there was any

## RUNNING FOR THE COACH

Punch and other hot spiced-wine drinks were an inseparable part of the Georgian coaching world that was rapidly displaced by the railroad after 1830. In their day English stagecoaches, like the one Pickwick and Tupman are racing to board, were the wonder of the world for their speed and reliability, regularly averaging ten miles an hour in ten-mile stages. Each stage began and ended at a tavern or inn, where fresh four-horse teams were put into the traces and passengers and crew refreshed themselves with a drop of something.

> orange peel in the punch, because orange peel always disagreed with him, and finding that there was not, Mr. Pickwick took another glass to the health of their absent friend, and then felt himself imperatively called upon to propose another in honour of the punch compounder, unknown.

The effect of six glasses (by our count) of cold punch upon Pickwick is impressive:

> Mr. Pickwick expressed a strong desire to recollect a song which he had heard in his infancy, and . . . sought to stimulate his memory with more

glasses of punch, which appeared to have quite a contrary effect; for, from forgetting the words of the song, he began to forget how to articulate any words at all. . . .

It is surely gin punch, too, that Sam Weller orders for the Bath footmen at their "swarry." He succeeds so well in "bringing them out" that the most dignified and arrogant of the lot, a footman in scarlet plush whom Sam calls "Blazes," ends the evening dancing the Frog Hornpipe on the table.

Whatever the other ingredients, deceit lurks in the punch served at Todger's boarding-house in *Martin Chuzzlewit*, where a great deal of archness attends upon its brewing, its maker protesting that "but for its color it might have been mistaken, in regard of its innocuous qualities, for new milk!" Mr. Pecksniff is quite taken in by it, and before long "spills a cup of coffee over his legs without being aware of the circumstance; nor does he seem to know that there is muffin on his knee."

Milk punch itself was a staple in the Dickens household, where guests noted that it (and toasted cheese) seemed inevitable at every meal. It may have reminded Dickens of the old coaching days, where at wayside stops everyone took "the great tumbler of fresh milk, one fair lump of sugar, two tablespoonsful of rum, and just a thought of nutmeg grating on the top of all." Milk punch figures powerfully in the post–chaise trip that Mr. Pickwick and his companions take from Bristol to Birmingham. Mr. Pickwick and Ben Allen are inside, while raucous Sam Weller and Bob Sawyer are in the "dickey" up behind, flying a red flag, blowing imaginary horns, and waving a case–bottle full of milk punch. "To serve them right," Mr. Pickwick and Ben drink it, every drop; and when they stop for lunch (at The Bell, Berkeley Heath) with bottled ale and Madeira, they have the case–bottle filled again. At The Hop Pole in Tewkesbury for dinner, with more ale, Madeira and some Port besides, it is filled yet again. Under the influence of milk–punch and etcetera, Mr. Pickwick and Ben sleep for thirty miles while Sam and Bob, unregenerate, sing duets in the dickey.

Of a post–chaise trip of his own, a junket through Cornwall in 1842 with a group of intimates, Dickens wrote:

If you could have seen but a gleam of the bright fires by which we sat in the big rooms of ancient inns at night, until long after the small hours had come and gone, or smelt but one steam of the hot punch (not white—like that amazing compound I sent you to taste of; but a rich genial glowing *brown*) which came in every evening in a huge brown china bowl!

## BY MILK PUNCH TO BIRMINGHAM

Well-to-do early Victorian travellers often eschewed stagecoaches and hired postchaises instead, light four-wheeled vehicles pulled by a team of horses with a postboy astride and with room for two passengers inside and two more outside, up on the "dickey" in back. On more than one occasion when he was a parliamentary shorthand reporter, Dickens rode all night in a postchaise to get election news back to his London paper, writing his story on a lap-board in the careening cab.

And from another letter,

> Heavens! If you could have seen the necks of the bottles, distracting in their immense varieties of shapes, peering out of the carriage pockets! If you could have witnessed the deep devotion of the postboys, the wild attachment of the hostlers, the maniac glee of the waiters! . . . I never laughed in my life as I did on this journey.

### BEDSIDE PUNCH AT DINGLEY DELL

After falling through the ice, Mr. Pickwick, ensconced in a fine old country four-post bedstead, takes the chair at a therapeutic bowl of punch or two or three, with the result that he is fit as a fiddle the next morning, thereby confirming Bob Sawyer's lofty view of the medicinal properties of the brew.

Writing at mid–century, Thackeray in *The Newcomes* looked back to 1825, when

> casinos were not invented, clubs were rather rare luxuries; there were sanded floors, triangular sawdust boxes, pipes and tavern parlors. Young Smith and Brown, from the Temple. . . . ordered their beefsteak and pint of port from the "plump headwaiter at the 'Cock' "; did not disdain the pit of the theatre; and for supper a homely refection at the tavern. How delightful are the suppers in Charles Lamb to read of even now!—the cards—the punch—the candles to be snuffed—the social oysters—the modest cheer! Who ever snuffs a candle now? What man has a domestic supper whose dinner–hour is eight o'clock?. . . . Many a grown man who peruses these historic pages has . . . only heard of rum punch as a drink his ancestors used to tipple.

By mid–century punch was no longer the "beverage which is peculiarly associated in our minds with the Roast Beef of Old England," in the words of Mr. Micawber. Cookbooks of the latter half of the century are stocked with recipes for all sorts of punches, including the old favorites, but there is a leaning towards Champagne and effeteness. One can imagine Sam Weller's comments on Punch a la Romaine, a mixture of meringued eggs, chablis syrup, frozen lemon juice, etc. Still, if that were the only punch going, Sam would have drunk it.

# Recipes

*Charles Dickens' Own
Punch,
18 January 1847*

*Juice and thinly peeled rind of 3 lemons; 2 good handfuls of lump sugar; 1 qt. boiling water; 1 pt. old rum; 1 or 2 large wineglasses brandy.*

Put rind, spirits, and sugar into a warm basin, and set fire to spirits by lighting a small quantity in a heated spoon and pouring in. Burn 3 or 4 minutes, stirring occasionally, then extinguish by covering bowl with tray. Add juice of 3 lemons and 1 quart boiling water. Stir, cover for 5 minutes, stir again and taste: add more sugar if desired. Pour all into large jug, tie thick cloth over top to exclude air, and keep warm until brought to table in a punch bowl. Also delicious when cooled by degrees and then iced. Less sugar is required for cold punch.

THE DICKENSIAN
1(1905), 205-06

*Garrick Club
Summer Gin Punch*

Founded in 1831, the Garrick was London's most important club devoted to "the patronage of the drama." As a member in good standing, Dickens may have enjoyed the club's famous summer gin punch, which was reputed to have been invented by his friend, Albert Smith.

*Juice and rind of 1 lemon, thinly pared; 1/2 pt. gin; 1 wineglass Maraschino; 1 1/4 pt. water; 2 bottles chilled soda-water.*

Pour gin on lemon peel in the bottom of a bowl, add lemon juice, Maraschino, water, and soda water.

Victorian recipes for cold gin punch are hardly more than variations on the above. Raspberry syrup was sometimes substituted for the Maraschino, and orange slices or a bit of pineapple might be added.

| | |
|---|---|
| *Flaming Green Tea Punch* | *1 oz. green tea; 1 qt. boiling water; 1/2 pt. brandy; 1/4 lb. sugar; juice and grated rind of 1 large lemon.* |

Make a strong infusion of the best green tea in the boiling water. Warm (by the fire if possible) a silver or other metal bowl until quite hot. Into it put the brandy, sugar, and lemon juice. Set these alight and slowly pour in the tea, stirring lightly with a ladle. The compound will remain burning long enough to fill the glasses. To heighten the flavor, rub the lemon rind on loaf or lump sugar.

| | |
|---|---|
| *Cold Tea Punch* | *Juice and grated rind of 1/2 lemon; juice and grated rind of 1 orange; 1 pt. rum; 1/2 oz. each of green and black tea; 2 1/2 lbs. sugar; 1 1/2 pt. water; 2 pts. arrack; 1 qt. soda water.* |

Macerate the fruit juices and grated rind in the rum and arrack for 24 hours, then strain. Make the two teas into 1 pt. of infusion by boiling in water for 15 minutes, then decant. Dissolve the sugar in the remaining water, combine, strain, and cool. Add ice-cold soda water to bowl at serving time.

If genuine arrack, an East Indian rum, cannot be found, steeping a head or two of flowers of benjamin in Jamaica rum overnight will produce a similar flavor, our sources affirm, and remark in passing that this is how the proprietors of Vauxhall Gardens probably forged their celebrated Rack Punch. A few drops of benzoic acid dissolved in a pint of rum should achieve the same result.

| | |
|---|---|
| *Quick Vauxhall Rack Punch* | *1 wineglass brandy; 1 wineglass Jamaica rum; 1 wineglass arrack; juice of 1/2 lemon; 1 tbsp. powdered sugar; boiling water.* |

Into a large tumbler or cocktail shaker pour the brandy, rum, arrack, lemon juice and sugar. Mix well, then drain into tumblers and fill with boiling water, stir, and serve.

**Regents' Punch**   *1 pt. strong green tea; rind and juice of 2 lemons; rind and juice of 2 oranges, one tart and one sweet; 1 bottle soda water, chilled; 1 pt. pineapple syrup; 1/2 lb. loaf sugar; small stick cinnamon; 1 bottle Champagne; 1/2 bottle Sherry; 3 wineglasses brandy; 1 wineglass each of rum, Noyau, and Curaçao.*

Combine tea, rind and juice of fruit, sugar, and cinnamon. Let stand for a half-hour, then strain, and add Champagne, Sherry, brandy, rum, Curaçao, Noyau, and syrup. Chill in a bowl, then add cold soda-water just before serving.

**Whisky Punch**   *Juice and rind of 1 lemon; 1/2 lb. powdered sugar; 1 pt. Scotch whisky; 2 glasses brandy; 1 qt. boiling water.*

Combine ingredients in warm bowl or jug and serve hot in stemmed glasses or goblets.

**Milk Punch**
" . . . *the milk–punch of human kindness.*"
*(Captain Marryat)*

*Juice and thinly pared rind of 12 lemons and 2 Seville or other tart oranges; 2 1/2 lbs. loaf sugar; 1 or 2 nutmegs, grated; 1 bottle pale brandy; 1 1/2 bottles old rum; 5 qts. water; 1 qt. scalded milk.*

Combine rind of fruit, brandy, rum, sugar, and nutmeg and let stand one week. Then add fruit juice, water, and, last, the scalded milk. Let stand one hour, then strain through jelly bags until clear. Bottle for later use. It will improve with age and may be served either hot or cold.

*Notes on Punch-making.* Our sources agree that hot punch is improved by the addition of a glass or two of Sherry or Noyau or a tot of Bay Rum. To "soften" a hot punch, add a pint of calves'–foot jelly or a tablespoon of guava jelly. Historians of punch agree with Dickens that an earthenware jug is the proper receptacle for brewing, especially since it can be stoppered with a clean napkin or kitchen towel and placed

on the hearth to allow the ingredients to mingle a few minutes before quaffing begins in earnest.

Our Victorian forebears enjoyed a much wider selection
of different types of rum than we moderns, running the gam-
ut from dark and heavy to light, whereas today distillers of
rum seem to have taken lighter spirits for their model.
With the exception of cold summer punches, which even
then were likely to employ the lighter rums, the drinks described above should be made in part at least with dark rums.
In most cities of the United States it may take some searching to find them, but we think it is worth the effort.

*Capillaire*. In place of sugar and water, old–time puncheurs
could count on having close at hand a quantity of sugar-
syrup they called capillaire. To make it, add seven pounds
of sugar to one gallon of water and put over a fire to simmer.
When warm, add the well–beaten white of an egg or two. As
these simmer with the syrup, skim well, and when thoroughly dissolved and reduced by half, pour off, flavor with
some Orgeat, and bottle for later use. In place of the egg
whites, some maidenhair fern may be placed in the bottles to
improve viscosity. The Orgeat may be omitted.

 Chapter Five

# *"Love–Itch"*

### DICKENS

Almost at the outset of Victoria's reign, the open indulgence of Georgian times gave way, if not to moderation, at least to a respectable hypocrisy. Excess did not die in 1837, but merely began to look pale and wear a black arm–band. Thus Mr. Pecksniff, in the days before the funeral of old Mr. Chuzzlewit,

> deeming that the mourner wanted comfort, and that high feeding was likely
> to do him infinite service, availed himself of these opportunities to such
> good purpose, that they kept quite a dainty table during this melancholy
> season; with sweetbreads, stewed kidneys, oysters. . . . over which, and
> sundry jorums of hot punch, Mr. Pecksniff delivered such moral reflections
> and spiritual consolation as might have converted a heathen. . . .

Amidst such "dismal jollity and grim enjoyment," with everyone feasting "like a Ghoule," Respectability could enjoy itself even as it fell into the fireplace and had to be carried kicking and preaching off to bed—it happens to Mr. Pecksniff on another occasion.

Even a little glass of sweet wine or cordial required its garland of deprecation and justification. " 'Lauk, Mrs. Bardell . . . see what you've been and done!' " cries Mrs. Cluppins, when Mrs. Bardell is so forgetful as to fill the ladies' glasses after filling Sam Weller's. " 'Ah, my poor head!' " says Mrs. Bardell—heaping coals on Mr. Pickwick's head, for everyone there knows that it is the breach–of–promise suit she is bringing against that innocent gentleman which has made her head "poor." This is so persuasive that Mrs. Sanders feels able to base a second round on it, only adding "that if she hadn't had the presence of mind to have done so, she must have dropped."

The ladies are drinking from a black bottle that could be cowslip wine, cordial, or liqueur, for these were the favorite restoratives of the Victorian sisterhood. "Whereas the toast most honoured among men is Wine and

Women, they should adopt as their own return toast—Men and Maraschino,"
as someone noted. Another feminine favorite was Curaçao—tropically romantic,
"sweet enough to catch flies," and strong—about 60 proof. Any lady who could
not openly savor such a sippable fell back in the arms of her retainers, and was
"reluctantly revived" with it, like Mrs. Veneering(OMF).

Mrs. Varden in *Barnaby Rudge*, who is a little like Catherine Dickens, gets
into a "highly spasmodic state" during a marital argument, forcing her husband
to give way at last,

> after a vast amount of moaning and crying upstairs, and much damping of
> foreheads, and vinegaring of temples, and hartshorning of noses, and so
> forth . . . assisted by warm brandy–and–water not over–weak, and divers
> other cordials, also of a stimulating quality, administered at first in
> teaspoonfuls and afterwards in increasing doses. . . .

"A DROP OF COMFORT"

Victorian social conventions forced women who wanted a drink into a host of
subterfuges to get one. Fortunately, female stereotyping provided a convenient
out—feminine sensitivity and susceptability—with the result that the least *con-
tretemps* could be plausibly converted into hysterics, a sinking spell, or the "fan-
tods," all of which required treatment with several doses of flavored and sweetened alcohol that might easily run above 150 proof.

Whereas liqueurs were imported, expensive, made from arcane ingredients with complicated—even secret—formulae, cordials were simple home–made infusions of common fruit in spirits. From the Latin *cor, cordis*, "pertaining to the heart," cordials were often administered when one's circulation needed restoring. Thus the Pickwickians are met with cherry cordial when they arrive, chilled after a wintry walk, at Manor Farm, probably made by steeping Kentish cherries, which were plentiful, in brandy, with some cherry leaves and cracked pits, and a little cardamom or mace. Currants, damsons, rhubarb, what not, were made into cordials in this way. The spices, like cardamom, cloves, ginger, mace, galangal, quassia, and cassia, were almost all tropical, but angelica grew in and about London and was sold in the streets by Seven Dials denizens. When sloe gin became popular in the eighties, the sloe bushes for twenty miles about London were stripped by the poor, who got sixpence a pound for the fruit.

What cordials and liqueurs had in common was sugar (plenty of it) and spirits, of course. "Capillaire" was the favorite sugar–syrup, made with triple-refined sugar and an infusion of maidenhair fern for viscosity; Dr. Johnson liked to add capillaire to his Port. The exoticism of liqueurs was often heightened by coloring and by unusual bottles. Wemmick in *Great Expectations* has one, "a black bottle with a porcelain-topped cork, representing some clerical dignitary of a rubicund and social aspect." In *Nickleby* the miser Arthur Gride has a shelf "laden with tall Flemish drinking glasses and quaint bottles, some with necks like so many storks; and others with square Dutch-built bodies and short fat apoplectic throats," from among which he selects "a dusty bottle of promising appearance and two glasses of curiously small size." This proves to be the miser's delight, "Eau d'Or," or Goldwasser, a golden, lemony liqueur with flecks of real gold leaf floating in it. In the *Canterbury Tales*, written at a time when alchemists associated gold with both the human heart and its cosmic counterpart, the sun, Chaucer ironically remarks of the richly dressed "Doctour of Phisik" that "For gold in phisik is cordial,/Therefore he lovede gold in special"—as physicians still do.

The illustrious Maypole Inn has "amazing bottles in old oaken pigeon–holes . . . [and] sturdy little Dutch kegs ranged in rows upon the shelves," while at the renowned Six Jolly Fellowship Porters tavern, there are "corpulent little casks and . . . cordial–bottles radiant with fictitious grapes." (Nowadays both grapes and casks are fictitious, if that is not too harsh a word for plastic.) These reappear in a letter of Dickens' to Leigh Hunt, in which he reminisces about a real–life inn called "Eel–Pie House," on the island of that name in the Thames at Twickenham:

Good God how well I know that room! Don't you remember a queer, cool, odd kind of smell it has, suggestive of porter, and even pipes at an enormous distance? Don't you remember the tea–board, and the sand, and the press on the landing outside full of clean linen intensely white? Don't you recollect the little pile of clean spittoons in one nook near the fireplace . . . like a collection of petrified three–cornered hats. . . . And closing my eyes, I'm down stairs in the bar where the soda water comes out of the window seat where the landlady sits o' fine evenings, where the lemons hang in a grove each in its own particular net, where "the cheese" is kept, with a great store of biscuits hard by in a wicker basket—where those wonderful bottles are, that hold cordials. You know 'em? great masses of grapes painted on 'em in green, blue, and yellow, and the semblance of an extraordinary knot of ribbon supporting the emblem of a label, whereon is the name of the compound? On one of these is "Lovitch." Great Heaven what is Lovitch? Has it any connection with peppermint, or is it another name for nectar? Tell me my heart, can *this* be Love–itch?

"Lovage" is the cordial referred to, as Dickens knew very well; it can still be found in England.

A pleasant beverage called "shrub" appeared during the reign of Queen Anne early in the eighteenth century; it was made with brandy, white wine, citrus juice and sugar, usually well in advance of need and left to collect its thoughts in the cellar. Mr. Snagsby, the hen–pecked law–stationer of *Bleak House*, offers a glass of placative Shrub to his termagant wife at a difficult moment. Servants such as the Bath footmen favored it, while public–school boys, according to Thackeray, tippled Shrub at their surreptitious "tucks."

In the *Sketches*, Miss Evans, her chum, and their gentlemen friends take Shrub at the Crown, Pentonville, and then, as we have seen, go on to the Eagle for rum and Sherry and caraway–seed biscuits and flirting. But the evening ends badly with the two girls going home in a hackney and a state of insensibility as a result of "shrub, sherry and excitement." Morleena Kenwigs in *Nickleby* is invited "to repair next day, per steamer from Westminster Bridge, unto the Eel–Pie Island at Twickenham, there to make merry upon a cold collation, bottled beer, shrub and shrimps ["srub" and "srimps" in the Cockney pronunciation] and to dance in the open air to the music of a locomotive [strolling] band." Eel–Pie Island was in favor for picnic parties then (1839), but by the time Dickens' son Charley wrote his *Dictionary of the Thames* (1839), it was "rather out of vogue"—as was Shrub itself, for that matter. The most pleasant scene involving shrub is in *Pickwick*, when on Christmas Eve they take it as a night–cap. A decoction called "Nectar" was typically made with raisins,

## THE "COSY" OF "THE MARQUIS OF GRANBY"

The Victorian "cosy" has evolved into the "snug" of the modern English pub, supposing that modernizing brewers have allowed any to survive. The cosy used to be a minute parlor replete with fireplace where *la patronne* kept watch and ward and into which specially favored friends like Mr. Stiggins might be invited. Whatever her faults, the second Mrs. Weller appears to have kept a "good 'ouse," to judge by the row of cordials above the bar.

honey, lemons and peel infused in boiling water, with Sherry, rum or other spirits added later. A placard for it appears in one of Phiz's illustrations for *David Copperfield.*

From medieval chatelaines down to Victorian housekeepers, English dames

## TWICKENHAM AIT

Better known as Eel-Pie Island, it was until very recent times a favorite up-river resort for
Londoners such as Morleena Kenwigs, who repaired there aboard a paddle-wheeler like that above
for shrub, the music of a locomotive band, and a little coquetting. The young Dickens knew it well,
but in later years he celebrated his wedding anniversary at the "Star and Garter" on the river at
Richmond, where gardens went down to the water.

kept in their still-rooms stores of condiments, preserves, medicines and
delectable homemade wines and cordials, as we see in *Edwin Drood*, where Mrs.
Crisparkle's closet is opened to our prying view:

> The upper slide, on being pulled down . . . revealed deep shelves of
> pickle-jars, jam-pots, tin canisters, spice boxes, and agreeably outlandish
> vessels of blue and white, the luscious lodgings of preserved tamarinds and
> ginger. . . . The pickles . . . announced their portly forms, in printed

capitals, as Walnut, Gherkin, Onion, Cabbage, Cauliflower, Mixed, and other members of that noble family. The jams . . . announced themselves in feminine calligraphy, like a soft whisper, to be Raspberry, Gooseberry, Apricot, Plum, Damson, Apple, and Peach . . . the lower slide ascending, oranges were revealed, attended by a mighty japanned sugar–box. . . . Home–made biscuits . . . a goodly fragment of plum–cake, and various slender ladies' fingers, to be dipped into sweet wine. . . . Lowest of all, a compact leaden vault enshrined the sweet wine and a stock of cordials . . . Seville Orange, Lemon, Almond and Caraway–seed.

In another closet she has "amazing infusions of gentian, peppermint, gilliflower (pink), sage, parsley, thyme, rue, rosemary, and dandelion . . . " Taverns of the period sold such infusions as "Gin–and–Rue," "Ginger–gin," "Damson Gin," and "Gin–and–Tansy," which has the most disarming recipe we have come across: "Put some Tansy in a bottle and fill it up with Gin." Gin–and–Cloves is taken as a "stomachic" at the Sol's Arms in *Bleak House*, and by Sam Weller and Job Trotter as a hang–over remedy. David Copperfield's tipsy servant has "a taste for cordials": gin–and–cloves and rum–and–peppermint (which she always charges to the account of "Mrs. C.").

Gin–and–peppermint appears in *Oliver Twist*, when Mrs. Corney, matron of the work–house, is taken queer:

> "Then take something, ma'am," said Mr. Bumble [the beadle] sooth-ingly. "A little of the wine?"
>
> "Not for the world!" replied Mrs. Corney. "I couldn't,—oh! The top shelf in the right-hand corner—oh!" Uttering these words, the good lady pointed, distractedly, to the cupboard, and underwent a convulsion from internal spasms. Mr. Bumble rushed to the closet; and, snatching a pint green–glass bottle from the shelf thus incoherently indicated, filled a tea-cup with its contents, and held it to the lady's lips.
>
> "I'm better now," said Mrs. Corney, falling back, after drinking half of it.
>
> Mr. Bumble raised his eyes piously to the ceiling in thankfulness; and, bringing them down again to the brim of the cup, lifted it to his nose.
>
> "Peppermint," exclaimed Mrs. Corney in a faint voice, smiling gently on the beadle as she spoke. "Try it! There's a little—a little something else in it."
>
> Mr. Bumble tasted the medicine with a doubtful look; smacked his lips; took another taste, and put down the cup empty.

"It's very comforting," said Mrs. Corney.

"Very much so indeed, ma'am," said the beadle.

Mrs. Corney's complaint is probably thirst, not hysteria or flatulence, but peppermint was thought to be sovereign for the latter two, at least.

Treats and treatments were sometimes indistinguishable. When Mr. Pickwick falls through the ice at Dingley Dell, he is packed off to bed, with a fire glowing in the bedroom grate; and a great bowl of punch is carried up. They "make the bed the chair," where Pickwick presides. More bowls are brought. And when Mr. Pickwick wakes the next morning there is not a symptom of rheumatism about him, which proves, as Mr. Bob Sawyer very justly observes, that there is nothing like hot punch in such cases; and that if ever hot punch did fail to act as a preventative, it was merely because the patient fell into the vulgar error of not taking enough of it. Bob Sawyer himself mixes punch with a pestle, in his Bristol apothecary shop:

> After dinner, Mr. Bob Sawyer ordered in the largest mortar in the shop, and proceeded to brew a reeking jorum of rum punch therein: stirring up and amalgamating the materials with a pestle in a very creditable and apothecary–like manner. Mr. Sawyer, being a bachelor, had only one tumbler in the house, which was assigned to Mr. Winkle as a compliment to the visitor: Mr. Ben Allen being accommodated with a funnel with a cork in the narrow end: and Bob Sawyer contented himself with one of those wide–lipped crystal vessels inscribed with a variety of cabalistic characters, in which chemists are wont to measure out their liquid drugs in compounding prescriptions. . . .
>
> There was no singing, because Mr. Sawyer said it wouldn't look professional. . . .

Alcohol was medically prescribed so often that Dickens retails a little joke about "the man whom the doctors ordered to get drunk once a month, and who, that he might not overlook it, got drunk every day." Mr. Omer, in *David Copperfield*, always takes Shrub–and–water when he smokes, as "softening to the passages," while Silas Wegg takes gin before reading aloud, to "meller the organ" in *Our Mutual Friend*. In *Hard Times*, Mrs. Sparsit urges Mr. Bounderby to take "sherry warm, with lemon–peel and nutmeg" before going to bed; and Bounderby comes back at her later with instructions to put her feet in hot water, when she is feeling low, while drinking "scalding rum–and–butter."

"Bring out the patent digester," says Bob Sawyer, meaning brandy. Bitters was the usual "digester," however, especially Angostura; but in Soho one could get "Swiss whets and drams" such as gentian bitters (two ounces of gentian root, one ounce of dried orange peel, a half–ounce of bruised cardamom seeds, infused in a full quart of brandy). Bitters frequently contained as much as fourteen parts of alcohol to one of water, yet Peruvian bitters was thought to cure drunkenness. Such potions were drunk daily, by people in good standing with Temperance societies, for grim happy–hours.

Many patent medicines had liquor in them and were duly called "cordials," "elixirs," or "liqueurs." "I do not know a better dram than Solomon's Balm of Gilead," declared Captain Marryat, who claimed to have assisted at an after–dinner "sitting" at which this medicine was drunk, after Champagne and claret, in lieu of brandy. "Godfrey's Cordial" (100 drops of laudanum per ounce, with treacle and sassafras) and the similar "Daffy's Elixir" were commonly used to pacify children. Since 1893 aspirin has come to replace many such remedies, the gentler sort at least, especially in the treatment of hangovers. Joseph Sedley in Thackeray's *Vanity Fair* tries beer after taking far too much Vauxhall Rack Punch the night before; but David Copperfield seems helpless after his maiden debauch: "Oh, what an evening, when I sat down by my fire to a basin of mutton broth, dimpled all over with fat. . . . " Some desperate men tried cider; but soda–water (after 1798) or barley–water was the commonest refuge. Bob Sawyer, whose pharmaceutical knowledge can't be denied, calls for soda water after that milk–punchy trip from Bristol to Birmingham, and Mr. Pickwick himself, as a natural philosopher, evinces "an unusual attachment to silence and soda–water" after a long sitting at the Bull Inn, Rochester.

When the latter visits the London law firm of Dodson and Fogg, one of the clerks is saying confidentially to another, " 'It was half–past four when I got to Somers Town, and then I was so uncommon lushey, that I couldn't find the place where the key went in, and was obliged to knock up the old 'ooman' "; whereupon he proceeds to mix up a Seidlitz powder under cover of his desk. All the famous spa waters were copied, including the "killibeate" (chalybeate) waters of Bath taken by Mr. Pickwick, that contain ferrous sulfate; " 'I thought they'd a wery strong flavour o' warm flat–irons,' " says Sam Weller. Ordinary soda–water was made by treating a quantity of marble dust with sulfuric acid and passing the resulting carbonic gas through purifiers into water. Sulfuric acid could "come over" in the generator, which was, at the very least, a poor remedy for an acid condition; and besides there were often traces of arsenic in the acid; Pickwick was well–advised to stick to brandy and plain water.

## SODA-WATER MACHINE

Here striking an attitude somewhere between boredom and self-importance, a Cockney soda-water man fills bottles with his homemade carbonated water, made by passing acid through marble dust, before venturing out into the streets to hawk his wares to passersby. After the perfection of the process by Schweppe in 1798, soda-water and other carbonated beverages became very popular, particularly as accompaniments to spirits. Victorian tipplers did not like to mix soda and spirits, however, preferring to take their brandy neat and follow it with soda.

The use of marble–dust led to a suspicion that "soda–water lay cold upon the stomach," as Dick Swiveller thinks, or even that it reverted to cement in one's insides. Thus Dick likes to qualify his morning-after soda–water with "ginger, or a small infusion of brandy." Brandy, all the spirits, and wine, bitters and cordials, were taken in experimental mixtures by sufferers who had had too much Dickensian celebration the night before: Sherry–and–bitters; "bin–and–jitters"; vermouth, perhaps with sloe–gin; gin–and–sloe–gin ("Slow and Quick"); Curaçao–and–brandy; or simply a straight dram. Gentlemen could try Champagne mixed with beaten eggs, bitters or brandy: "The Boy," an Anglo–Indian pick–me–up surely known to Thackeray and Major Bagstock. Egg–nog (with brandy and madeira); brandy–and–beef–tea; orange–wine–and–sulfate–of–quinine; and brandy–with–half–a–lemon's–juice–and–a–strong–dash–of–cayenne–pepper ("The Scorcher") were also favored. Hot pickle sandwiches (toast spread with chopped West Indian pickles) and "Devilled Biscuit" (a cheese biscuit spread with a paste made of finely ground lobster–meat, butter, mustard, ginger, cayenne, Chili vinegar, salt and a little curry–powder) were on the mustard–plaster plan, pitting one misery against another.

Lower down the social scale, a porter in the Southwark hop–markets could go to the Red Cross Tavern and call for "a 'alf-quatern o' Twist": equal amounts of rum and gin, a simple homeopathic remedy. Or a navvy might buy a red herring from a costermonger, cut it up raw with his clasp–knife, and wash it down with porter or a go of gin–and–peppermint. "The Pump" (putting your head under it) was a last resort, which Dickens mentions in connection with Sam Weller, among others. Mr. Stiggins' involuntary baptism in the horse–trough is but an extreme, total–immersion case of this practice.

These are still familiar devices, but the Victorians had an idea that drunkenness itself might be cured by taking preventatives. We have mentioned Peruvian bitters in this regard, and herbs such as lousewort (wood betony) and colewort (a cabbage–like plant), "as much as will lie on a sixpence," were also recommended as a daily regimen. The following recipe, however, probably tells us why the preventative notion has disappeared: gentian, cardamom, centaury, and steel filings, infused in white wine. In the latter part of the century a host of new foaming potions were developed, containing various carbonates and tartaric or citric acid. The rise of the American bar in London, and the evolution in America itself of the soda–fountain, swiftly produced a pharmacopoeia of sweet, fizzy "ales, beers, cordials, flips, grogs, liqueurs,

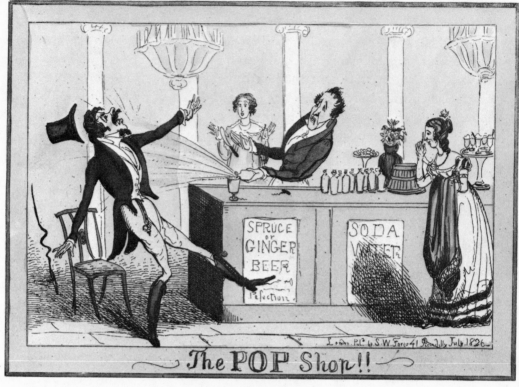

The POP Shop!!

## "THE POP-SHOP"

Early attempts at carbonation were not always dependable, and accidents sometimes spoiled the "turn out" of Regency dandies such as the one depicted above, who prided themselves on the impeccable cleanliness and tight fit of their ensembles. Sometimes also the toxic acids from which soda water was made "came over" in the process of manufacture and poisoned an unlucky customer, prompting wary tipplers like Dick Swiveller to avoid it altogether as being "heavy on the stomach."

nectars, punches, shrubs and syllabubs" that kept alive the names if not the spiritous reality of the old drinks.

But the future lay across the Atlantic: in 1900 a fizzy drink with both caffeine and a form of cocaine was recommended by American apothecaries for "nervous persons, brain workers, and persons who have been bicycling. "It was called a "Kola-coca Cordial."

**Shrub**

*1 gal. new milk, scalded; 2 qts. red or white wine; 2 gal. rum; 1 gal. brandy; finely pared rind of 6 lemons and 4 Seville or other tart oranges; juice of 12 lemons and tart oranges; 3 lbs. sugar.*

Combine all ingredients except sugar and let stand for 24 hours. Add sugar, stir to mix well and keep in covered jug for two weeks. Strain and bottle.

**Lovage**

*1 gal. gin; 1 pt. capillaire; 1 lb. freshly cut celery–root; 1 oz. sweet fennel; 1 drachm oil of cinnamon; 30 drops oil of caraway seeds.*

To the gin and syrup mixture, add a tincture made by macerating the celery–root and fennel in pure spirit for two days. Add oils of cinnamon and caraway and strain clear (or stand clear). Bottle for later use.

We find it hard to understand why celery–root should have been substituted in this recipe for the genuine article, which is often found in English gardens and can be seen in American gardening centers. Leaves, stems, and seeds of lovage, an easily grown perennial, may be used to flavor this formidable cordial. It tastes like celery, to be sure, but a celery that has died and gone to heaven.

**English Rum Shrub**

*3 gals. Jamaica rum; 1 qt. orange juice; 1 pt. lemon juice together with thinly pared rind; 6 lbs. icing sugar; 3 pts. scalded milk.*

Mix rum, orange and lemon juices, lemon rind, and sugar. Cover tightly overnight. Then scald the milk, and when it has cooled, pour it into the spirit and juice mixture. Mix the whole thoroughly, let it stand for an hour, and then strain through a flannel bag lined with blotting-paper. Bottle for later use.

*Angelica Liqueur*

*1 oz. finely chopped angelica stem; 2 pts. brandy; 1 oz. skinned bitter almonds pounded into a pulp; 1 pt. capillaire.*

Steep the ingredients in brandy for five days, then strain through fine muslin and add sugar syrup.

Or: Pour 1 qt. boiling water on 6 oz. angelica root, thickly sliced, and infuse for 1 1/2 hours. Strain. Add juice of 2 lemons, 4 oz. honey, and 1/2 gill brandy. Mix well and bottle.

*Orange Brandy*

*1/2 gal. brandy; 3/4 pt. Seville orange juice; 1 1/4 lb. sugar; rind of 2 or 3 Seville oranges grated on sugar cubes; thinly pared rinds of 6 Seville oranges.*

Combine brandy, orange juice, and sugar. Grate in the orange rind and add the pared rind. Let all stand in a covered container three days, stirring 3 or 4 times a day. When clear, it should be bottled and closely corked for a year. It will then be ready for use, but it will keep any length of time.

*Usquebaugh*
*(The best was made at Drogheda, in Ireland.)*

*1 gal. good brandy; 1 lb. raisins; 1 lb. brown sugar candy; 1 oz. each powdered nutmeg, cloves, cinnamon, and cardamom; 1/4 oz. saffron; finely pared rind of 1 Seville orange.*

Combine all the ingredients in a large jar and shake well once a day for three weeks at least. Then filter and bottle for later use.

*Eau d'Or*

*30 drops oil of lemon; 5 drops oil of mace; 3 drops oil of cinnamon; 48 oz. alcohol; 60 oz. sugar; distilled water to make 1 gallon.*

Dissolve the oils in the alcohol and the sugar in the water, mix the solutions, add yellow coloring, filter clear and add some tiny bits of gold leaf. Bottle.

*Eau d'Argent*   Violet petals (fresh), lemon juice, angelica, cloves, anise, sugar, alcohol, and water, with rose coloring and bits of leaves of silver: combine as above.

*Golden Slipper*   In a fancy wineglass, combine the yolk of an egg in half a wineglass of yellow Chartreuse and half a wineglass of Eau d'Or in such fashion that the egg and the liqueurs do not mix.

*Gin–and–Pine*   Split the dark heart of a green pine log into fine splints about the size of a lead pencil; take two oz. of the same, and put into a quart decanter, then fill the decanter with gin. Let the pine soak for two hours. Decant and bottle.

*Gin–and–Tansy*   Fill a quart decanter one–third full of tansy and top off with gin. Steep for a month, then decant and rebottle.

*Gin–and–Rue*   To one pint of good English gin add 1/2 pint of rue sprigs nicely picked and washed. Steep for one month, then decant and rebottle.

*Gin–and–Wormwood*   Put three or four sprigs of wormwood into a quart decanter and fill with gin. Steep for a month before using.

*Pick–Me–Up*   Put into a small tumbler six drops of Angostura Bitters, one-third of a liqueurglass each of Curaçao, yellow Chartreuse, and brandy. Stir well with a spoon and serve in a wineglass.

*Twist*   "This," says one of our sources, "is a favorite liqueur of porters in the hop-warehouses. You go into the "Red Cross," for instance, and ask for a ' 'alf-quartern o' Twist in a three–out glass,' and you will find that it consists of equal parts of rum and gin, and is a powerful pick–me–up after a wet night."

*Prairie Oyster*
*(original version)*

Into a tumbler crack one raw egg, add malt vinegar and salt and pepper to taste. Take in one gulp.

*Prairie Oyster*
*(later version)*

Into a tumbler crack one raw egg. Add a tot of one's favorite spirit or whisky, Worcestershire sauce, Tabasco, and bitters. Take in one gulp. (Optional: add tomato juice or beef bouillon and drink more slowly.)

It was such a concoction prepared by Jeeves to heal the prostrate Bertie Wooster after a long evening at the Drones Club that earned him his on–the–spot appointment.

*A Caveat to Would-Be Cordial Makers*: When the recipes above mention "alcohol," something approximating pure medical alcohol (200°) seems to have been meant.

Chapter Six

# "*Blue Ruin*"

The native English drinks that Shakespeare knew were beer, cider, perry, mead, and country wines made from berries and flowers such as the freckled cowslip. A grape wine of sorts was made at Ledbury in Norman times, but Falstaff's wine was all imported: sack, malmsey, rhenish, "Bordeaux stuff" or claret, and "Canaries, that marvelous searching wine." Drunkenness existed, of course, and men died of it, but mass alcoholism did not arrive until the advent of distilled spirits, especially gin. Or until the advent of "the Masses" themselves: for in the seventeenth and eighteenth centuries London and the northern industrial cities were filling up with displaced farm workers, who had been pushed off the land by new agricultural techniques and land enclosures. The proletarian misery and poverty they endured required a powerful anodyne. By 1740, when corrective legislation was enacted, gin–drinking had reached such epidemic proportions that it threatened to exterminate the urban working–class— witness Hogarth's "Gin Lane."

A hundred years later the dependency of the poor on gin and other spirits was still a problem. Dutch gin, French brandy, West Indian rum, and whisky (Scottish "yell" and Irish "potheen") contributed less to the problem than English gin since, being imported and a bit more complicated to make, they were more expensive. But gin was made in England from cheap neutral spirit that could be distilled anywhere from anything—literally from garbage—and the flavorings were native and plentiful. In Dickens' time a quarter of a pint, or "quatern," of gin cost three-pence and was quite enough to knock a starving man out on the straw provided by some "gin–spinners," as the proprietors of gin-shops were called. "The thin-armed, puffed-faced, leaden-lipped gin-drinkers," or "bingo-boys" on a "gin crawl," lived almost entirely on gin toward the end. "Bung-eyed" when they left the "sluicery," they slept it off for an hour or two, and then came in for another dram, regular as clock-work—"For all who wake to cry or grin / Find comfort in a drop of gin," as the comic song had it.

### "THE DRAM-DRINKER"

The Temperance Movement was a reaction to scenes like this, familiar to every Victorian, which threatened to drown the urban proletariate in alcohol. Dickens argued that Teetotalers only attacked the symptoms and failed to address the deeper social disease. The child waiting for her half-pint bottle to be refilled with gin reminds us that during Dickens' lifetime restrictions on drinking by children were few or none.

Victorians were afraid of gin partly because they were afraid of the poor, a terror fostered by the French Revolution and its aftermath, the Terror. The "Gin Scare" of the 1820s occurred when the consumption of spirits doubled immediately following a dramatic reduction of duties in 1825; and a fourfold increase in the number of criminal convictions in London between 1811 and 1827 was widely blamed on gin. In *Barnaby Rudge* Dickens paints a dreadful picture of a Gordonite mob gathered around a pool of flaming spirits that formed in the street during the spoiling of a vintner's house, lapping it up even as they burn. Another mob bursts into the Maypole Inn looking for drink and loot. In *A Tale of Two Cities* it is a wine–cask that has broken open in the street, and a maddened mob of Parisian poor who feverishly scoop it up, "even champing the moister wine–rotted fragments" of the cask.

The Temperance Movement of the 1840s was given added stimulus by talk of Chartism and revolution. To wean the mob from gin seemed necessary on humanitarian grounds; but also to some Victorians it appeared a useful preventative of social unrest, a strategy more to their liking than true reform. Dickens disagreed entirely with the Teetotalers' approach to the problem, whatever their motivation, and in an article of 1848 attacking it he made clear that he thought urban misery and poverty were the causes of gin–drinking, and should themselves be eradicated. Already in *Sketches by Boz* he had written:

> Gin-drinking is a great vice in England, but wretchedness and dirt are a greater; and until you improve the homes of the poor, or persuade a half–famished wretch not to seek relief in . . . temporary oblivion . . . gin–shops will increase in number and splendour. If Temperance Societies would suggest an antidote against hunger, filth, and foul air . . . gin–palaces would be numbered among the things that were.

But "gin–palaces" and "wine–vaults" were just then in their heyday. It needed little capital outlay to go into the gin business: a man could rent a cellar in a slum court and make up a distillate of sawdust, vegetable refuse or cotton rags, flavored with angelica (common in London brickfields) and juniper. He cut this with water from such sources as the Tower Hill ditch, over which hung a line of jakes, while to disguise the bad taste and weakness he might add sulfuric acid (with traces of arsenic in it) and cayenne pepper (already adulterated with red lead). After a year or two of selling out the back door, his capital would have increased encouragingly; he could then rent a shop, and set up a bar, perhaps with perforations through which spilled gin ran through lead pipes into hidden bottles to be sold again. As soon as the profits permitted, he would lease a larger shop at the corner of a teeming intersection, decorate extravagantly, as we shall see, and open a proper "palace."

Such places were the first to open before dawn, when the streets were filled with laborers going to work, fish–sellers, farmers with donkey–carts full of produce and livestock, drovers with their herds, milkwomen with pails—"an unbroken concourse of people," many of whom would stop in for a dram or a go to keep out the chill, or instead of breakfast. "Gin palaces, like hell, ever open to a customer," as Marryat wrote. The brewers' drays were lumbering in from

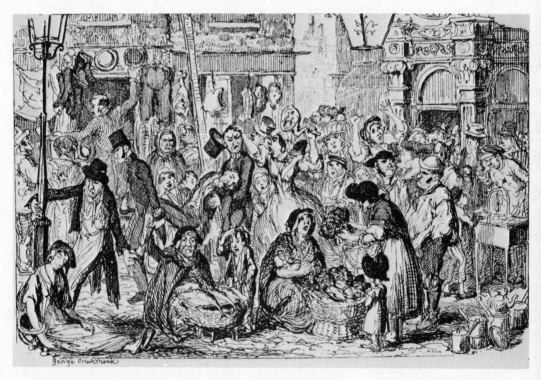

### "*LOW* SUNDAY"

A street scene in front of a gin-palace before the first Sunday Closing laws were enacted in 1839, when gin-shops, splendid in stuccoed neo-classical façades and huge, ornate gas-lamps, were round-the-clock operations. Since pubs and gin-shops often served as hiring-halls, pay-offices, and loan-shops, unscrupulous employers and publicans conspired to enforce a kind of wage-slavery based on gin, rather like the company stores of mining towns.

Southwark, the red-capped draymen, having already had one eye-opener, ready for another. Clerks streamed by from Somers Town and Kentish Town, looking to start their day off right as well. At night the human tide turned, and the streets and public-houses were busier than ever, everyone eager for a "digester," a "topper-offer," or "to make a night of it." There were few other entertainments. At corner locations the glare from several ginshops made the whole intersection lurid, and served the theatrical uses of pie-men, hot-potato-men, men carrying sandwich-boards, a dozen in a row ("Now for the Kali-bonca Root!"), and prostitutes posing and ambling.

Behind its façade often lay abject poverty, tenements packed from basement to attic with indigent "families," eight or ten people to a room, existing in hopeless squalor:

> The filthy and miserable appearance of [the Seven Dials slums] . . . can hardly be imagined. . . . Wretched houses with broken windows patched with rags and paper . . . filth everywhere . . . clothes drying and slops emptying, from the windows; girls of fourteen or fifteen, with matted hair, walking about barefoot, and in white great-coats, almost their only covering . . . men and women, in every variety of scanty and dirty apparel, lounging, scolding, drinking, smoking, squabbling, fighting and swearing.
>
> You turn the corner. What a change! All is light and brilliancy. The hum of many voices issues from that splendid gin-shop which forms the commencement of the two streets opposite; and the gay building with the fantastically-ornamented parapet, the illuminated clock, the plate-glass windows surrounded by stucco rosettes, and its profusion of gas-lights in richly-gilt burners, is perfectly dazzling when contrasted with the darkness and dirt we have just left. The interior is even gayer than the exterior. A bar of French-polished mahogany, elegantly carved, extends the whole width of the place, and there are two aisles of great casks, painted green and gold, enclosed within a light brass rail, and bearing such inscriptions as "Old Tom, 549"; "Young Tom, 360"; "Samson, 1421"—the figures agreeing, we presume, with "gallons," understood. (*Boz*)

In back of the bar with its elaborate back-fittings and bevelled mirrors, "showily-dressed damsels with large necklaces" presided, under the eye of the "diddle cove," "a stout, coarse fellow in a fur cap." Baskets of Palmer's biscuits and plates of stale pies and sandwiches covered with wickerwork line the counter.

George Cruikshank

## GIN-SHOP

Inside, gin-shops' tawdry splendours continued, providing the only light, luxury, and gaiety in the drab lives of the Victorian poor and offering oblivion at threepence a quartern. Cruikshank, who was all too familiar with gin-shops himself, captures the vivacious scene: flaring gas-lamps, pretty barmaids, tuns of "Out-and-Out" and "Cream of the Valley," and raucous company. To the right a burly pugilist keeps a look-out for trouble, which appears to be brewing across the room.

. . . [T]wo old washerwomen . . . receive their half-quatern of gin and peppermint, with considerable deference, prefacing a request for "one of them soft biscuits," with a "Jist be good enough, ma'am. . . . " The young fellow in a brown coat and bright buttons . . . calls for a "ker-vorten and a three–out–glass," just as if the place were his own. . . .

Three people could order two drinks to be divided into three glasses, hoping thereby to get an extra measure: that was a "kervorten in a three–out–glass." Mr. Pecksniff and Jonas Chuzzlewit try this in a tavern on the road from Wiltshire to London, by ordering two six–pennyworths of spirits instead of one shillingsworth. "Kervorten" is Cockney for "quatern," a quarter of a pint. Gin itself had the short, mocking nicknames that narcotics always have: "bingo," "max," "Jacky," "crank"(gin–and–water), "cogue" (a dram of gin), and "shove–in–the–mouth."

> By many names dear gin is called:
> "Strip me naked" is by porters bawled;
> "Flash of lightning" th' amorous spark;
> The dandy asks for "Nancy Clark."

Terms like "stark–naked," "white port," "white wine," "fuller's earth," and "white tape" referred to the colorless gin itself—the latter also implying the clear stream of gin flowing from the bottle, as in "Give me a yard of tape." The greyish–white skin of the bingo–boys is suggested in "white face," and "dead white." "Blue tape" and "blue ruin" point to gin–poisoning, that made drunkards' faces "a ghostly, ghastly corpse–like kind of blue," according to Walter Besant. The nickname "deadly" came from the gin made by Deady and Co., while a "squail of South Sea Mountain" meant a dram of gin.

The so-called "wine–vaults" were an early form of the modern departmented liquor store, but with consumption encouraged on the premises. The departments were marked with handsome ground–glass lettering: "Brandy Bell," "Whiskey Entrance," "Wine Promenade." The Gin Department was large, with colorful placards announcing "Butter Gin," "The Out and Out," "The No Mistake," "The Good for Mixing," "The Regular Flare-up," and "The Real Knock–Me–Down," according to the *Sketches*. "Young Tom" and "Old Tom" were sweetened gins, while "Christmas gin" was probably ordinary gin sold during the Christmas season. The prices varied: Mr. Krook, the rag-and–bottle dealer of *Bleak House*, asks for "the Lord Chancellor's fourteen-penny" gin, but naturally likes the "eighteen–penny" better, when any "no-bleman" or "baron of the land" will treat him to it.

Good, strong gin was available, for a price or through a connection, for the usual sort came in by night from Holland. Dickens was probably hinting at such "jigger stuff" in a letter: "I have discovered that the landlord of the Albion [on the Kentish coast] has some delicious Hollands." Perhaps this was Schiedam, like the very strong gin that Quilp shares with Dick Swiveller in *The Old Curiosity Shop*. Dick, being used to "crank," has to throw part of his away and fill up with water before he can take it. On rare occasions Sam Weller takes "British Hollands": gin made in England by the Dutch method.

Hollands gin is sometimes taken as one takes brandy, after dinner with coffee and cigars. Thus at the annual dinners of the Worshipful Company of Cloth-workers guests are served with noggins of gin and brandy, with the inquiry, "Do you dine, Sir, with Alderman or Lady Cooper?" This custom goes back to a dinner of 1684, when Alderman Cooper, while a guest of the Company, was seized with apoplexy, plied with brandy, and expired. It was the Company's fault, Lady Cooper maintained, for not having any Hollands: that would have brought him round right enough. She established a fund for the Company to provide both brandy and Hollands ever afterward to be sure it never happened again; and sure enough, it hasn't.

The comic songs of the free–and–easies often had gin as their subject:

> The Cream of the Valley is fled,
>     The taste of its once lusty shower
> From my throat for a month it has sped;
>     For my blunt is all gone—oh ye powers!
>
> To daffy shops for luscious drops
>     Folks stalk in now so numerous,
> And soak their clay with sweet, sweet gin,
>     And jest and joke so humorous.

Such songs were popular, along with worse ones, at low taverns like the Three Cripples, Saffron Hill, where Sikes and Fagin take their rouse:

> The room was illuminated by two gas–lights; the glare of which was pre-vented by the barred shutters, and closely–drawn curtains of faded red, from being visible outside. The ceiling was blackened, to prevent its colour from being injured by the flaring of the lamps; and the place was  . . .  full

of dense tobacco smoke. . . . [There was] a numerous company, male and female, crowded round a long table: at the upper end of which, sat a chairman with a hammer of office in his hand; while a professional gentleman, with a bluish nose, and his face tied up for the benefit of a toothache, presided at a jingling piano in a remote corner. . . . Near [the chairman] were the singers: receiving, with professional indifference, the compliments of the company, and applying themselves, in turn, to a dozen proffered glasses of spirits and water . . . Cunning, ferocity, and drunkenness in all its stages, were there, in their strongest aspects; and women: some with the last lingering tinge of their early freshness almost fading as you looked: others with every mark and stamp of their sex utterly beaten out . . . some mere girls, others but young women, and none past the prime of life. . . .

*Oliver Twist* is very much a gin–drinking novel. Oliver himself is born in a poor–house, and accidentally baptized in gin by the crone who attends his birth. Later, when Oliver falls in with Fagin's gang of youthful pickpockets, he finds they all drink gin, and the girls too, who are prostitutes. And Oliver begins to drink gin himself, in just the way children of the poor did begin: he is given warm gin–and–water by Fagin to put him to sleep. Babes in arms were given rags soaked in sweet gin to stop their crying; and it was common to see youngsters taking ale as Oliver does at Barnet, where every other house was an alehouse, or leaving a gin–shop dead drunk at midnight. Ninetta Crummles, the child performer of *Nicholas Nickleby*, is "kept up very late every night . . . on an unlimited allowance of gin–and–water" to prevent her growing tall.

Children born in workhouses and prisons found their way back as adults, and gin went with them. Spirits were illegal in prison, but there were "whistling shops," as Mr. Pickwick learns:

> "What is that, Sam? A bird–fancier's?" inquired Mr. Pickwick.
> "Bless your heart, no, sir . . . a whistling-shop, sir, is where they sell spirits."

It appears that when a search is to be made by prison authorities, " 'the turn-keys knows before hand, and gives the word to the wistler, and you *may* wistle when you goes to look for it.' " A "tiddly-wink," on the other hand, was an unlicensed ale- or spirits–shop.

Compared to the indulgent *Pickwick Papers*, *Oliver Twist* must have partly pleased Temperance enthusiasts, for drink is damned in it by association with

## "THE FREE AND EASY"

"The Three Cripples" of *Oliver Twist* was a typical low ale-house or gin-shop in the Saffron Hill district and a criminal hang-out, as may be inferred from the glimpse of Fagin entering at the rear, behind the man with toothache at the piano. A "harmonic evening" is far enough along for one member of the company, at least, to have succumbed to his transports.

some very ugly people. But gin is not actually blamed for the evils exposed in *Oliver*; the worst punishment is reserved for Bill Sikes, who is sober when he murders Nancy, and for Fagin, whose evil–doing owes nothing to drink or to social injustice in any ordinary sense.

Even in *Oliver* Dickens could not resist endowing some of his tippling types with a naughty charm—something a Teetotaler would never have done. Mrs. Mann, the matron of the baby farm where Oliver is boarded out, offers Mr. Bumble, the "parochial beadle," "a little drop of somethink," for example, but Bumble refuses according to protocol:

> "Not a drop. Not a drop," said Mr. Bumble, waving his right hand in a dignified, but placid manner.
>
> "I think you will," said Mrs. Mann, who had noticed the tone of the refusal . . . . "Just a leetle drop, with a little cold water, and a lump of sugar."
>
> Mr. Bumble coughed.
>
> "Now, just a leetle drop," said Mrs. Mann persuasively.
>
> "What is it?" inquired the beadle.
>
> "Why, it's what I'm obliged to keep a little of in the house, to put into the blessed infants' Daffy, when they ain't well, Mr. Bumble," replied Mrs. Mann as she opened a corner cupboard, and took down a bottle and glass. "It's gin. I'll not deceive you, Mr. B. It's gin."

Daffy was a nickname for gin, but here it means a pacifier containing laudanum.

An indulgence of naughtiness—"Pickwickedness"—was the tone in which Dickens "brought out" many of his bibulous comic–Olympians: Micawber, Stiggins, Pecksniff, and of course Samuel Pickwick himself. None of these deities is really designed for salvation by either Temperance or Reform, but to be savored, although they sometimes get their come–uppance, of course. Reform of any sort is inconceivable in the dainty presence of Sarah Gamp, the everything–drinking nurse of *Martin Chuzzlewit*, spreading upon the breeze when she goes a-visiting "a peculiar fragrance . . . as if a passing fairy had hiccoughed, and had previously been to a wine–vaults." Sairey has an unseen friend, Mrs. Harris, who "often and often" praises Mrs. Gamp's moderation— or so that lady tells us herself:

> " 'Sairey Gamp,' she says . . . 'never did I think till I know'd you, as any woman could sick–nurse and monthly likewise, on the little you takes to drink.' 'Mrs. Harris,' I says to her, 'none on us knows what we can do until

## A TEAPOT OF GIN

Sairey Gamp and Betsy Prig share a teapot of gin shortly before Betsy's doubts about the substantial existence of Sairey's imaginary friend Mrs. Harris precipitate a permanent rupture in their relationship. The gin in question was no doubt something sweet like "Old Tom" or "Cream of the Valley."

we tries . . . my half a pint fully satisfies; perwisin', Mrs. Harris, that it is brought reg'lar and draw'd mild.' "

But in the middle of a nice sit–down over a teapotful of gin, Mrs. Gamp is horrified to hear her colleague Betsey Prig declare crushingly that " 'there's no sich a person' " as the hypothetical Mrs. Harris. As Sairey says later, " 'The words she spoke of Mrs. Harris, lambs could not forgive, nor worms forget.' "

Several other Dickens' figures follow Mrs. Gamp in mingling spirits with tea–time; Mrs. Jarley of the "Waxworks" spikes her tea with brandy in *The Old Curiosity Shop*, as does Flora Finching in *Little Dorrit*, modelled on an old flame of Dickens who had developed the same habit in her disappointing middle–age.

In "London Recreations" (*Boz*), Dickens shows us a family on an outing at a "tea–gardens," eating prawns and winkles and judiciously taking tea first and

## "THE SPANIARD'S" TEA GARDENS

Mrs. Bardell and her friends take tea in the well-known Hampstead watering hole, one of dozens of tea gardens spotted around London's inner suburbs during the novelist's youth, where tea was likely to be followed, or accompanied, by "somethink stronger"—a tot of gin "warm with," "just to keep the cold out." Mr. Jackson from Dodgson and Fogg's office and his friend, a process-server, take "something short"—a hooker of gin—before arresting Mrs. Bardell for debt.

gin afterwards, " 'just to keep the night air out, and to do it up comfortable and rigler arter sich an as–tonishin' hot day!' " In *Pickwick Papers* the spot chosen is The Spaniards, Hampstead Heath, which fortunately survives and even has a small "gardens" in the rear. Mrs. Bardell and her friends get there by "cabriolly," for tea and "something short" afterwards, probably gin–and–water "without *all* the water," as Bertie Wooster says to Jeeves. Gin with warm water and sugar was simply "warm–with," while gin and cold water without sugar was "cold–without." In *Nicholas Nickleby* the name "Baron von Koeldwethout of Grogzwig" masks three East–London favorites: "cold–without," "grog," and "swigg," a noun meaning liquor or a sip of liquor.

Another delight was an evening at White Conduit House, Pentonville, known far and wide (in the East End, anyway) as "Vite Condick." To sing at Condick seems to have had the same allure for early–Victorian shop–girls as dancing at the Moulin Rouge would later have for the laundresses of Montmartre. Amelia Martin is "The Mistaken Milliner" (*Boz*) who tries out there, before a short–suffering audience composed of 97 gins–and–water, 25 bottled ales, 32 brandies–and–water, and 41 Neguses. The gins–and–water take the lead, naturally, in hissing Amelia off the stage.

As the years passed, it must have seemed that both Dickens and Cruikshank were right: the combination of Temperance efforts, social reform, and wise legislation led to a gradual lessening of spirits–drinking among workingmen and a corresponding increase in the consumption of malt beverages. As gin ceased to be "kill-soul" it became socially more acceptable. Dickens often served iced gin punch and gin slings to his guests at Gadshill (where in honor of Falstaff nothing but sack should have been drunk) while they played badminton, croquet, and "leaping poles." For later–Victorian mixed drinks gin became—what Mr. Venus says it is (*OMF*) as he tries to explain to his crony Silas Wegg how he makes "Cobbler's Punch":

> "It's difficult to impart the receipt for it . . . because, however particular you may be in allotting your materials, so much will depend upon the individual gifts, and there being a feeling thrown into it. But the groundwork is gin."

## ❧ Recipes

**Gin Fix**

Into a tumbler put a teaspoonful of icing sugar, half a wineglass of water, the juice and peel of a lemon, and one wineglass of gin. Shake well. Pour into a tumbler two-thirds filled with shaved ice and decorate with berries of the season. Serve with a straw.

A *Gin Sour* is made with the same ingredients, but omits all fruit except a small piece of lemon, the juice of which is squeezed into the glass.

**Gin Sling**

Combine in a tumbler thirty drops of gum syrup or a teaspoonful of icing sugar, half a wineglass of water, one wineglass of gin, and a small lump of ice. Stir well and dust with grated nutmeg.

(Gum syrup appears to be a combination of a simple sugar syrup or capillaire with a little gum arabic, which our forebears employed to increase viscosity.)

**Gin Fizz**

Put into a tumbler the juice of half a lemon and one wineglass of gin. Fill with shaved ice, shake well, and strain into a glass. Add a teaspoonful of icing sugar in which is placed a pinch of carbonate of soda. Stir again and drink while it effervesces.

**Gin Smash**

Combine in a tumbler one teaspoonful of sugar, half a wineglass of water, and one wineglass of gin. Shake well and pour into a glass two–thirds filled with shaved ice. Decorate with two sprigs of spearmint, two slices of orange, and berries in season. Serve with a straw.

**Pineapple Julep**

Put a slice of peeled pineapple into a cocktail shaker or large tumbler with the juice of half an orange, ten drops each of Maraschino and raspberry syrup, and half a wineglass of gin.

Shake well, pour into a glass filled with shaved ice, and add a quarter of a pint of Champagne. Decorate with berries of the season, and serve with a straw or two. (A quarter of a wineglass of pineapple syrup may be substituted for the fruit.)

## Gin Sangaree

Into a tumbler put one teaspoonful of icing sugar, one wineglass of gin, and half a wineglass of water. Shake well and pour into a glass two–thirds filled with shaved ice. Dash with Port wine and dust with nutmeg.

## Eye–Opener

Combine in a tumbler half a wineglass of Hollands gin, twelve drops of Angostura bitters, and thirty drops of gum syrup or a teaspoonful of icing sugar. Add shaved ice, shake, and pour into a glass.

## Gin Cocktail

Pour into a tumbler three dashes of simple syrup, two or three drops of Boker's bitters, one wineglass of Hollands or plain gin, one or two dashes of orange Curaçao, and a twist of lemon peel. Shake well and pour into a glass one-third filled with shaved ice.

## Ladies' Blush

*(Advertised by our sources as "a favorite drink among the fair sex.")*

Combine in a tumbler a wineglass of Old Tom gin, one teaspoonful of Noyau, and five drops of Absinthe or Pernod. Sweeten to taste with about one teaspoonful of white sugar. Shake well with shaved ice, strain, and pour into a colored glass, the rim of which has been damped with lemon juice and dipped in white sugar.

# Chapter Seven

# "Jamaikey, The Inwariable, and The Cratur"

The cheapest spirit next to gin was rum, and whatever prestige it enjoyed (aside from its use in rum–punch) was due to the British Navy. Many Englishmen had been on some sort of ship, if only the Margate steamer, and had seen sailors taking their ration of rum–and–water. Dickens found the sight so edifying he thought Temperance people ought to see it:

> I think it would do them good to smell the rum under the circumstances. Over the grog, mixed in a bucket, presides the boatswain's mate, small tin can in hand. Enter the crew, the guilty consumers, the grown–up brood of Giant Despair, in contradistinction to the band of youthful Angel Hope [a temperance group]. Some in boots, some in leggings, some in tarpaulins . . . most with sou'wester hats, all with something rough and ragged around the throat; all dripping salt water where they stand; all pelted by weather, besmeared with grease, and blackened by the sooty rigging.

After tossing off their rum–and–water, the sailors go back on deck "vastly comforted . . . even to the circulation of redder blood in their cold blue knuckles. . . ." Of course few people begrudged sailors their ration; it was what Jack Tar did with rum ashore that won disapproval. Nevertheless, grog (rum–and–water) became widely popular among lubbers.

Whereas gin–and–water was called "crank," meaning "sickly," "grog" was named after doughty Admiral Edward "Old Grog" Vernon, who wore a "grogram" (grosgrain) cloak at sea. In 1745 "Old Grog" introduced the practice of cutting the navy rum ration with water, supposedly to make it a more sociable ritual. Ashore, on the other hand, grog was used to mean any spirit, with water hot or cold, with or without sugar. Rum was at home "down by the

docks, [where] scraping fiddles go in the public–houses all day long, and shrill
. . . rises the screeching of innumerable parrots. . . ." It is grog that old
Barley, the retired ships' purser of *Great Expectations*, growls for from his bed of
gouty pain, at Millpond Bank, Chink's Basin, down along the Old Green
Copper Rope–walk between Greenwich and Limehouse. Captain Cuttle in
*Dombey* has similar tastes and lodgings, on a little canal near the India Docks
where "there is nothing to be smelt but rum and sugar" emanating from "rows
of public–houses with flagstaffs."

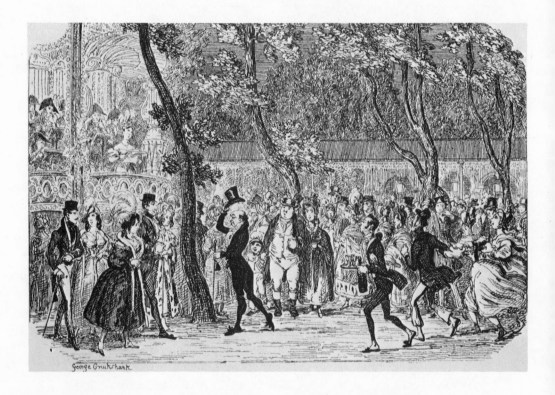

## VAUXHALL GARDENS

This famous Georgian pleasure grounds was on its last legs in the 1830s, when Dickens described its faded glories as seen by the cold light of day. But at night, its trees illuminated by
thousands of lights, it was a glamourous place indeed, though patrons joked about the thinness of
the slices of ham and the doubtful authenticity of its rack punch, here being carried by a waiter to a
party in one of the boxes surrounding the bandstand.

Navy rum was the dark Demerara type, but the most popular rum ashore was made in Jamaica, from the cane whose Latin name, *Saccharum officinarum*, may have provided the name. Shipped to England in large oak puncheons, it was laid down for five to seven years in the vaults under the docks of London to age, before blending and bottling. It was from the West India docks that "The Reverend" Melchisedech Howler in *Dombey* got himself discharged for "screwing gimlets into the puncheons and applying his lips to the orifice," whereupon he "announced the destruction of the world for that day two years, at ten in the morning . . . and opened a front parlour for the reception of ladies and gentlemen of the Ranting persuasion." His sermons were so effective "that in their rapturous performance of a sacred jig . . . the whole flock broke through into a kitchen below, and disabled a mangle belonging to one of the fold."

And all because of "London Dock Jamaica Rum." Silas Wegg of *Our Mutual Friend* likes "a sociable glass of old Jamaikey warm," singing " 'we'll take a glass with a slice of lemon in it to which you're partial, for auld lang syne.' " To save space rum was sold in "case–bottles" of dark green glass with flat sides; bright green was used for gin-flasks, giving the name "bottle–green" to the jackets favored by sportsmen like Mr. Winkle. Daniel Quilp, the villainous dwarf of *The Old Curiosity Shop*, has a large case–bottle of Jamaica rum, which he sometimes drinks boiling hot, to the discomfiture of guests like Samson Brass who have to share it with him. In the same novel, Dick Swiveller is treated on one occasion to some "extraordinary" and "amazing" rum, which was probably smuggled, over–proof stuff. This raises a thirst in Dick that requires several "modest quenchers" afterwards at his pub. "Modest Quencher" was an in–joke in Dickens' male circle, having reference to a certain cool young lady as well as to drinks, just as, for obvious reasons, rum was known as "O–B–Joyful."

That old fraud, the Reverend Mr. Stiggins, though loudly asserting that " 'all taps is wanities,' " admits readily to Sam Weller that the wanity he " 'likes the flavour on best [is] the liquor called rum—warm, my dear young friend, with three lumps of sugar to the tumbler.' " Particularly, he favors very sweet and hot pineapple rum–and–water:

> Mr. Stiggins . . . looked about him, rubbed his hands, wept, smiled, wept again, and then, walking softly across the room to a well–remembered shelf in one corner, took down a tumbler, and with great deliberation, put four lumps of sugar in it. Having got thus far, he looked about him again,

## QUILP'S GROG

The grotesquely sinister Quilp takes his boiling hot rum and water with a
cigar. Rum is the oldest of all distilled spirits, following on the heels of the
introduction of sugar-cane into Europe by Alexander the Great and the perfection of distillation by the Arabs early in the middle ages. Cultivation of sugar-
cane and the production of rum from its molasses made the Caribbean Islands
worth fighting for during the seventeenth and eighteenth centuries.

and sighed grievously; with that, he walked softly into the bar, and pres-
ently returning with a tumbler half full of pine-apple rum, advanced to the
kettle which was singing gaily on the hob, mixed his grog, stirred it, sipped
it, sat down, and taking a long and hearty pull at the rum-and-water,
stopped for breath.

The next instant Mr. Weller has him by the collar, and with violent kicks
(interrupted only to adjust his hat), propels Stiggins out the inn-door and into
the house-trough.

"There!" said Mr. Weller, throwing all his energy into one most complicated kick . . . "send any vun o' them lazy shepherds here, and I'll pound him to a jelly first, and drownd him artervards! Sammy, help me in, and fill me a small glass o' brandy. I'm out o' breath, my boy."

Pineapple–rum—that is, rum in which chunks of pineapple had been soaked—was quite a favorite in the Dickens household, where dozens of bottles of it reposed among the fine wines. As for Mr. Weller, his "inwariable alleviator" is brandy, which shows that he is what Dickens called "a steady old boy":

> There was once a fine collection of old boys to be seen round the circular table at Offley's every night, between the hours of half–past eight and half–past eleven. We have lost sight of them for some time. There were, and may be still, for aught we know, two splendid specimens in full blossom at the Rainbow Tavern in Fleet Street, who always used to sit in the box nearest the fireplace, and smoked long cherry–stick pipes which went under the table, with the bowls resting on the floor. Grand old boys they were—fat, red-faced, white-headed old fellows—always there—one on one side of the table, and the other opposite—puffing and drinking away in great state. Everybody knew them, and it was supposed by some people that they were both immortal.

John Dounce, in *Sketches by Boz*, is such an old boy:

> . . . Regular as clockwork—breakfast at nine—dress and tittivate a little—down to the Sir Somebody's Head—a glass of ale and the paper—come back again, and take daughters out for a walk—dinner at three—glass of grog and pipe—nap—tea—little walk—Sir Somebody's Head again—capital house—delightful evenings.

If Dounce and his cronies go to the theater there is "none of your hurrying and nonsense"; they have their brandy–and–water first comfortably, and order a steak and oysters for supper to be eaten later. Unfortunately, this pleasant routine is upset one night when Dounce happens in at an oyster house where there is a pretty girl in attendance. She not only opens his oysters but goes to the public–house for his liquor as well, "and back she comes, tripping over the coal–cellar lids like a whipping–top, with a tumbler of brandy–and–water, which Mr. John Dounce insisted on her taking her share of, as it was regular ladies' grog—hot, strong, sweet, and plenty of it." Dounce is smitten, gives up

### THE OLD BOY

Any venerable regular at a London tavern
was an "old boy" like John Dounce, who
could depend on getting the same table every
night, the same drinking companions, the
same glasses of brandy/rum/gin-and-water-
warm-with (in that order of social acceptabil-
ity), and the same churchwarden, which
might be long enough for its bowl to rest
upon the floor under the table.

his old friends and makes himself ridiculous—all for a young lady who
" 'wouldn't have him at no price.' " Whereupon he marries his cook on the
rebound, "with whom he now lives, a hen–pecked husband . . . and a living
warning to all uxorious old boys."

Brandy, or "Red Ribbon," went with good cigars, devilled anything, native
oysters, and the fast life of London's smart set, Victorian style. Lesser men,
hoping to be tarred delightfully with that brush (such as Montague Tigg, on his
way to becoming Tigg Montague, Esquire), affected brandy even when they
could hardly afford it (MC). Bill Sikes, who as a burglar has a reputation to keep

up, prefers "Jack Dandy" (rhyming slang for brandy) when he wants to "have a drop in the eye," while Nancy, the girl who shares his bed, and who is herself a prostitute, typically likes gin, or "Samson." Another "Samson" was a mixture of brandy, cider, sugar, and water, and "Cock–a–Doodle Broth" was brandy–and–water combined with sugar beaten up in eggs.

Much better known, of course, is Mr. Samuel Pickwick, M.P.C., natural philosopher with two monographs to his credit and a learned society named in his honor. Almost the first thing Mr. Pickwick does, after appearing in Goswell Street that innocent May morning in 1827, is to get his eye blacked, after which

## PICKWICK AND THE WELLERS IN A LONDON TAVERN

Aldin's illustration tells us much about the sociology of Victorian drinking. Mr. Pickwick's party has the best box in the house—that is, the one closest to the fire—and Pickwick, as a gentleman, occupies the best seat in the box, for the same reason. Even though we know that Tony Weller's "inwariable" was brandy-and-water, he and Sam have been given pints of porter, while Mr. Pickwick enjoys the gentleman's drink, hot, with sugar and lemon.

he takes the first of many glasses of brandy–and–water. This time it is on Mr. Jingle's advice: " 'Glasses round,—brandy–and–water, hot and strong, and sweet, and plenty. . . . ' " and Jingle shows how to do it by swallowing "at a draught full half–a–pint of the reeking brandy–and–water . . . as if nothing uncommon had occurred." Later, Mr. Pickwick finds ample occasion to say " 'Let us celebrate . . . with a convivial glass!' " whereat the Pickwickians devote the rest of the evening to brandy and conversation with their leader in the chair. On one occasion, when he can't stomach the Port at the Great White Horse Inn, Ipswich, he orders brandy instead—but if the Port were bad, the brandy was probably no better. The bar brandy that so many Dickens figures take would have been frequently stale and tainted; at the worst, it was often adulterated or faked outright, with a compound of oil of cognac, ammonia, strong black tea, prunes, crushed prune pits and rose leaves in spirits, according to "Bacchus." Such brandy was called "ball o'fire," "cold tea," "French Cream," or "Nantz." This was the "brandy" put into the brandy–balls that were "going off like smoke" around Cook's Court, Cursitor Street, in *Bleak House*, following Nemo's death.

"Patent brandy" took its name from the "Patent" column still, in which neutral spirits were distilled from grain; this was mixed with ordinary French brandy and flavored with the fruit of one's choice: Dickens mentions "Orange Brandy," for instance. Henry Brett of Furnival's Inn, where Dickens lived for a time, was the maker of a popular sort: "Brett's Improved," held to be "congenial to the human stomach."

Hot brandy–and–water with grated nutmeg causes a notable coughing fit in "Mrs. Lirriper's Legacy," while a Spanish red wine called "tent" was sometimes added to brandy to make "Coke–on–Littleton," from the two legal authorities, one of whom wrote a commentary on the other. Ale and brandy was known as "Humpty–Dumpty"; and "Blood and Thunder" was Port mixed with brandy. But usually Victorians tempered ecstasy with caution, brandy with "splash." Water was the common splash; Charles Lamb liked cold water from the Hare Court pump with his many brandies. Brandy and water or soda was also the "inwariable" beverage for "making a night of it." Dickens' clerks Potter and Smithers, out on a tear, might find their way to a wine–vault, where there were "a good many young ladies, and various old gentlemen, and a plentiful sprinkling of hackney coachmen, all drinking and talking together" (prostitutes with prospective customers and pimps, most likely). They drank "small glasses of brandy, and large glasses of soda" until the night was "made" and they had gotten thoroughly "foxed." (Not until later in the century were the two mixed together to make a "B–and–S," however.) After the eighteen–seventies, brandy was hard to come by due to phylloxera, the dreaded disease of European wine grapes, and gave way to the modern taste for whisky. Irishmen were the drinkers who used and misused whisky most in Dickens' early days in London. As late as 1875, Gilbey's sold almost twice as much Irish whisky as Scotch, while Bourbon came over much later, and in small quantities. "A drap o' the cratur" was as common a request in the gin–shops of St. Giles as "a knock over the liver of the old gemman," as gin was called by the Irish. Elsewhere in London, especially in the West End, Scotch was available but expensive. As a young man, Dickens invited special friends in for Scotch and cigars, a combination he enshrined in the *Sketches*, where his errant clerks ask for "goes" of the best Scotch, and the "very mildest" cigars, after their dinner in the Strand (perhaps at Simpsons?). They mix their grog, and puff and toast themselves sound asleep at the table. Dickens favored "Isla" Scotch, which is

Och ! Judy dear, a fig for beer,

The pleasure sure is greater,

When you are dry, to bung your eye

With quarterns of the " cratur !"

## "THE CRATUR"

After the phylloxera epidemic wiped out European vineyards in the 1870s, brandy was hard to come by and of poor quality, and English topers turned to Irish and Scotch whiskies. "Potheen," as Irish whisky is still called, may rival rum in antiquity, and Celtic farmers may have developed the art of distilling as early as the Arabs. A "short and splash" remains the gentleman's preferred pub swig.

the best perhaps of four types: Highland, Lowland, Campbelltown, and Islay. Most Englishmen knew so little about whisky, however, that they were often bilked by hotel-keepers, who made a "whisky" of neutral spirit flavored with creosote and fusel oil.

Dickens' pleasantest reference to Scotch occurs in *Pickwick*, in the tale of

## A TOAST TO SOLOMON PELL

After a modest lunch of roast beef and raw oysters washed down with quarts of porter, Sam and Tony Weller and their coachman friends switch to brandy and water to salute the legal machinations of Pell, who has managed the business of getting Sam jailed for debt so that he may protect his master, who is already in "the Fleet." After a stop at another tavern on the way, the party delivers Sam to the prison doors in a mellow mood indeed.

"The Bagman's Uncle," who spends a day and a night on the town in Edinburgh. He begins with a substantial breakfast, and later refreshes himself with a light lunch of a bushel of oysters, a dozen or so of bottled ale, and a couple of noggins of Scotch to top off. Thus fortified, he moves on to a supper of kippers, finnan haddocks, and a haggis "like a Cupid's stomach," followed by whisky–toddy and song. The latter was one written by Robert Burns after a most convivial visit with his friend William Nicol: "Oh, Willie brewed a peck o' maut, / and Rob and Willie came to pree: / Three blyther hearts, that lee-lang night, / Ye wadna find in Christendie."—and so on for several verses. Then there is more whisky–toddy, and a whisky neat to prevent the toddies from disagreeing with him; and after that the bagman's uncle sees and hears quite remarkable things.

But on a tour of the Highlands, Dickens also saw the sorrier side of Scottish whisky-drinking on the way to Inverness, at an inn where there were fifty Highlanders, "all hopelessly and irreclaimably drunk . . . lying about in all directions: on forms, on the ground, about a loft overhead, round the turf–fire wrapped in plaids, on the tables, and under them." This was the reality behind the popular image of the Highlands, whose erstwhile proud clansmen were in Glasgow, Nova Scotia, or far–off Indiana, still singing nostalgically, "Here's to the land o' the butter and brose."

Athol Brose, which Charley in "The Holly–Tree" also remembers fondly, was a sort of caudle made with oatmeal, brown sugar, cream and Scotch or Drambuie. We can recommend a Southern New England counterpart, made with real maple syrup, Bourbon whisky and tapioca—from which deliberative guests have been known sometimes to drop the tapioca and syrup.

Scotch–Irish emigrants to the New World also brought with them their taste for malt whisky, the skills of distilling, and a settled antipathy to "revenooers," which, together with Indian corn, produced the Whiskey Rebellion and thereafter good Pennsylvania rye and Kentucky Bourbon. The latter took its name from the county where it originated, and made its way back to the Old World, in the form of Mint Julep.

**Hot Spiced Rum**

Combine in a tumbler one or two lumps of sugar, half a teaspoonful of mixed allspice, one wineglass of Jamaica rum, and a piece of fresh butter as large as a chestnut. Fill the tumbler with hot water and grate a little nutmeg on top before serving.

**Grandfather's Nightcap**

*1 gill old rum; 1 dessertspoon honey; 1/2 tsp. porter spice; 1 egg, separated; 1 oz. sugar; 1 lemon slice; hot water.*

Beat egg yolk, add porter spice, and stir in rum. Melt sugar in a cup with a tablespoon of boiling water and add to rum and egg, whisking all the while. Strain into a warm stemmed glass. Whip egg white until stiff and float on top. Serve with a spoon.

*Grandmother's Nightcap* substituted gin for brandy. (So much for grandmother!)

**Porter Spice**

*1 lb. bruised cloves; thinly pared rind of 6 lemons; 1/2 lb. bruised cinnamon; 2 oz. coriander seeds; 1/2 oz. bruised caraway seeds; 1 lb. allspice.*

Shake all ingredients over a fire until hot, then put in a gallon jar and fill with spirit. Let stand two weeks, shaking vigorously daily, then filter into a large crock. Add two gallons of sugar syrup or capillaire, and cork tightly for later use. A teaspoon may be added to flavor a pint of porter.

**Brandy Toddy**

Combine in a tumbler one teaspoonful of sugar, half a wineglass of water, a wineglass of brandy, and a small lump of ice. Stir with a spoon. For a hot Brandy Toddy use boiling water instead of ice.

Whisky or gin may be employed in place of brandy, together with a teaspoonful of sugar, a slice of lemon, and a stick of cinnamon. Then it is called a Hot Toddy and is a good housewife's specific for the *grippe*.

(A mixture of equal parts of Bourbon, honey, and lemon juice makes an excellent cough syrup.)

*Fixes, Fizzes, Sours,*
*Smashes, and Slings*

A *Fix* is a Toddy with the juice and peel of citrus added and served on cracked ice or with boiling water. It is decorated with berries in season. Rum, whiskey, or brandy may be used. A *Sour* is made like a Fix, except that the fruit is omitted and either Sherry or Champagne substituted for spirit. *Slings* are like Sours but lack citrus and use water instead of ice. *Smashes* are Juleps on a small scale; that is, a wineglass of any spirit on crushed ice, with a little icing sugar and water. The compound is shaken and poured into a glass or cup decorated with a slice of citrus and a sprig or two of spearmint. A *Fizz* is like a Sour except that citrus juice is added and a pinch of carbonate of soda is dropped in just before serving as an effervescent, thus:

*Morning Glory Fizz*

Dissolve in a little water the white of a fresh egg, and add the juice of half a lemon, 12 drops of lime juice, 30 drops of Absinthe or Pernod, and a wineglass of Scotch. Mix well. Just before serving add a pinch of carbonate of soda to make it effervesce.

*Golden Fizz*

Combine in a tumbler a wineglass of gin, juice of half a lemon, and cracked ice. Then the yolk of an egg is broken into the mixture, it is well shaken and poured out into a glass. Finally, a pinch of carbonate of soda is added. Serve.

*Burnt Brandy*
(*"A curious recipe from*
*Switzerland," one of our*
*sources says.*)

Cut the top off a lemon and hollow out the interior. Place the empty cone thus formed by the skin on top of a large wineglass. Fill the cone with brandy, rum, or whiskey; then balance a piece of sugar on the prongs of a fork, set the spirit

alight, and hold the sugar over the flame until it has melted
into the cone. Then pierce a small hole in the bottom of the
cone with a skewer. When all the spirit has trickled into the
glass, throw the cone away and drink the result.

*Swizzle*　　　Half–fill a small tumbler with crushed ice, then add 1 1/2
liqueurglasses of Boker's bitters, half a wineglass of brandy,
and two or three drops of Noyau. Now swizzle this mixture,
preferably with an Indian cane swizzle, to a froth. Serve with
a straw.

*Criterion Cocktail*　　　Mix together three–eights of a bottle of brandy, half a
pint of water, one liqueurglass of Boker's bitters, one wineglass of simple syrup, and half a liqueurglass of Benedictine.
Whisky or gin may substitute for brandy, and the mixture
may be bottled, and later poured over crushed ice in a shaker
before serving in a small tumbler. Or it may be strained into
a wineglass with a piece of lemon peel, the edge of the glass
first moistened with lemon juice and dipped in sugar.

*Brandy Champerelle*　　　Mix in a small tumbler one wineglass of brandy, six drops
of Angostura bitters, and a liqueurglass of Curaçao, with
shaved ice. Shake well, strain, and serve.

*Bull's Milk*　　　Put into a large tumbler one teaspoonful of icing sugar,
with half a pint of milk, one–third of a wineglass of Jamaica
rum, two–thirds of a wineglass of brandy. Add shaved ice,
shake well, strain into a large glass, and dust with cinnamon
and nutmeg.

*Auld Man's Milk*　　　Put into a tumbler with crushed ice two teaspoonfuls of
icing sugar, one egg well beaten, a quarter of a pint of fresh
milk, and a wineglass of Scotch whisky. Shake well, strain
into a glass, dust with nutmeg, insert two straws, and serve.

**Whisky Cobbler**    In a large tumbler or cocktail shaker with crushed ice combine two wineglasses of Irish or Scotch whisky, one tablespoonful of icing sugar, and two or three slices of orange. Shake well and strain into a glass. Decorate with slices of orange and clusters of grapes, and serve with two straws. (Any red wine may be substituted for the whisky. When Bourbon is used together with a little lemon juice, it becomes a Saddle Rock. A Monongahela omits the lemon juice.)

**Colleen Bawn**    Combine in a tumbler one egg beaten with a teaspoonful of sugar, one-third of a wineglass each of Yellow Chartreuse, Benedictine, and rye whisky. Shake well, strain into a glass, and dust with cinnamon, nutmeg, and pink sugar.

**Home Ruler**
*("A favorite drink at the bars of the House of Commons, during the reign of the Uncrowned King," say our sources.)*

Two well–beaten egg yolks are placed in a large tumbler with a little sifted sugar, and a small tumblerful of hot milk is gradually stirred in. Last of all a large wineglass of "John Jameson" is added.

**Black Stripe**    Combine a wineglass of Santa Cruz rum and a tablespoon of molasses. As a summer drink add a tablespoonful of water and crushed ice; as a winter drink fill up the tumbler with hot water. Grate a little nutmeg on top in either case.

**Tom and Jerry**    Beat the whites of six eggs to a stiff froth and the yolks until they are "as thin as water," then mix them together in a punch bowl with a quarter wineglass of Jamaica rum, two pounds of icing sugar, and a teaspoonful of mixed spice (nutmeg and cinnamon), until the mixture attains the consistency of a light batter. Put a tablespoonful of this mixture into a small tumbler with a wineglass of brandy, and nearly fill with boiling water. Serve with a dusting of nutmeg. (A little carbonate of soda mixed into the batter will prevent the sugar from settling to the bottom.) Also, a mixture of one pint of brandy and half a pint each of Jamaica rum and white or Santa Cruz rum may be made up ahead of time, and substituted for the brandy. For cold Tom and Jerry use cold milk.

*Pineapple Rum*

Steep some chunks of freshly sliced pineapple in a bottle of rum for a month, then decant the liquid for use in a drink made of equal parts of the flavored rum and hot water, with sugar to taste. Pineapple and rum share an ester in common, which makes this wedding an especially felicitous one.

*Robert Burns'*
*Hunting Flask*

*Grated rind of 2 lemons; 1 oz. bruised ginger; 1 qt. Irish whisky; 1 lb. sugar; 1 lb. ripe white currants.*

To the whisky add lemon rind, ginger, and currants. Put in a covered vessel and let stand a few days. Strain carefully and add sugar. Bottle two days after for later use.

We cannot understand why the poet and bibulophile Bobbie Burns should have forsaken his beloved Scotch for Irish whisky in this recipe, but it should be intuitively obvious even to the most casual observer that this potation will keep one warm in the field.

# Chapter Eight

# "*Native Pewter*"

BOB SAWYER

To encourage the "lower orders" to drink beer instead of gin and other spirits, the Crown in 1836 remitted the beer-tax; with good results, for it halved the price of beer and encouraged more and more workingmen to agree with Joe Gargery (GE): " 'Wot a pipe and a pint of beer do give refreshment to the working-man, Sir, and do not over-stimulate.' " Joe is not above accepting a glass of rum, however, " 'Once in a way, and on a Saturday night, too.' " And ale was alcoholic too, of course. Here is Sarah Gamp, whom we have already met drinking gin, ordering up her late supper, and some very strong ale, from the chambermaid of the private house where she is "sick–nursing":

> "I think, young woman," said Mrs. Gamp . . . in a tone expressive of weakness, "that I could pick a little bit of pickled salmon, with a nice little sprig of fennel, and a sprinkling of white pepper. I takes new bread, my dear, with jest a little pat of fresh butter, and a mossel of cheese. In case there should be such a thing as a cowcumber in the 'ouse, will you be so kind as to bring it, for I'm rather partial to 'em, and they does a world of good in a sick room. If they draws the Brighton Tipper here, I takes *that* ale at night, my love; it being considered wakeful by the doctors." (MC)

As we have seen, Gamp likes her ale "brought reg'lar and draw'd mild." To draw ale "mild" meant to fill the pot slowly so as to get as little foam and as much ale as possible. Dickens wrote in a business letter long afterward, "I likes my payments to be made reg'lar, and I likewise likes my publishers to draw it mild." He was always as "punctual and particular" about money matters as Sairey is about her drink, who required

> a pint of mild porter at lunch, a pint at dinner, half–a–pint as a species of stay or holdfast between dinner and tea, and a pint of the celebrated stagger-

ing ale, or real old Brighton Tipper, at supper; besides the bottle [of spirits]
on the chimney-piece, and such casual invitations to refresh herself . . .
as the good breeding of her employers might prompt them to offer. (MC)

In 1753 a Dr. Russell stimulated the popularity of Brighton by advocating
ocean bathing, and even suggested drinking sea-water for the health. A nearby
brewer, however, Thomas Tipper, knew a trick worth two of that: he drew hard
water from seaside wells to brew the "celebrated staggering ale" known to Mrs.
Gamp as "The Real Old Brighton Tipper." This was the sort of "hard" ale
advertised by placards in wine-vaults, for which, as Dickens put it, "the poet's
art has been called into requisition, to intimate that, if you drink a certain
description of ale, you must hold fast by the rail." The ale was still sold in 1856,
when an ad for it appeared in *The London Illustrated News*: "Christmas Ales.—
The Celebrated BRIGHTON TIPPER Ales, Old and Mild, in 9 and 18
gallon casks. . . . Hallet and Abbey's Brighton Ale Stores, Hungerford."
Sairey likes her Tipper "old," rich and strong, as does the Game Chicken (DS),
the boxer who trains on old ale and beefsteaks. "Stunning" was another term for
strong ale, as "genuine" was for home-brewed. David Copperfield asks a London landlord,

> "What is your best—your *very best*—ale a glass?"
> . . . "Two-pence-halfpenny," says the landlord, "is the price of the
> genuine Stunning Ale."
> "Then," says I, producing the money, "Just draw me a glass of the
> Genuine Stunning, if you please, with a good head to it."

But he is so small that the landlord hesitates to serve him, asking many ques-
tions. David finally receives ale—probably neither Stunning nor Genuine, he
thinks later—and his money back and a kiss from the landlady into the bargain.
(This real-life episode took place at The Red Lion, Derby and Parliament
streets, when the twelve-year-old Dickens, his parents briefly jailed for debt,
had to endure the humiliation of labor in a shoe-blacking factory.)

Beer is everywhere in Dickens: at rowing-matches on the Thames; at the
Crown and Anchor ball-room, Greenwich Fair, where men and women dance
on each others' hats; at the workhouse, diluted; in the ordinaries of Bucklers-
bury, propping up clerks' newspapers; at the Eagle Tavern and white Conduit
House, borne about by rushing waiters; at "harmonic gatherings" of shabby-
genteel men in City ale-houses; at seaside hotels in Yarmouth, Ramsgate,
Gravesend, and Margate; as "half-and-half" in slap-bangs and for servants'

## THE POTMAN

This scene of the infamous London slum, Seven Dials, indicates the prominence of gin palaces, marked by gigantic gas-lamps over their doors, and potmen, such as the one at right carrying two loaded trays of pints of "heavy wet" porter, in the lives of the Victorian proletariate. A neighborhood notable, the potman not only delivered the mealtime pot of beer to nearby households but also served as a local authority-figure, clearing-house of news and local gossip, pub-bouncer and general factotum, and nemesis and victim of street-urchins. In large establishments the potman's menial duties of collecting and cleaning pots were delegated to the potboy, usually a much-oppressed youth.

suppers in country houses. Bob Sawyer likes it "in its native pewter." Even Bill Sikes, fleeing from the murder of Nancy, "does a pint," with bread and meat, at a suburban tavern.

When we first meet Tony Weller, the rubicund coachman, he is burying as much of his face as will fit in a quart pot, while his son Sam takes a pull that causes the old gentleman to stare and say, " 'Wery good power o' suction, Sammy . . . you'd ha' made an uncommon fine oyster if you'd been born in that station o' life.' "

Home–made ale, called "stingo," was still to be found throughout the Victorian countryside in Dickens' youth, when "the rector's wife knew exactly how much malt went into every barrel of Hall ale," as Thackeray says. Rural taverns were often farm–houses originally, where the "ale–wife" or "Mother Red Cap" brewed good stingo. Her husband, on his way to becoming a "jolly landlord," would partition off a corner of his kitchen, where ordinary guests were entertained, for storing barrels, with a dutch door for serving. This became the "tap–room," while more genteel guests were served in the "parlor" adjoining; and other rooms were taken over as business grew. Dickens describes some such arrangement at the Six Jolly Fellowship Porters in London (OMF): the tap-room is tiny, full of beer–pulls (invented in 1810 by Joseph Bramah of Bramah-Lock fame), casks and cordial–bottles, lemons in nets and biscuits in baskets, with the landlady's supper–table by the fire. This snug bar was "divided from the rough world" by a glass partition and a half–door with a leaden sill, where customers like Rogue Riderhood stood to their drink in a dark and draughty passageway. In the parlor there are "red curtains matching the noses of the regular customers" and a fireplace equipped with utensils for mulling ale and wine, as we have already seen. Opposite the bar is "a very little room . . . on the door of which is . . . painted its alluring name: COSY."

Even when an ale-house gave up brewing on the premises, it probably served local ales, such as Winchester Pale and Brunswick Mum (an imported German beer recommended by Knight), Alton ale (Thackeray in *Barry Lyndon*), Dorchester ale (Smollett in *Humphry Clinker*), Welsh ale (served at the London Coffee House by landlord John Leech, the father of Dickens' illustrator for *A Christmas Carol*), or "the hard ale of Wiltshire," fondly called to mind by Dickens himself in "The Holly–Tree." ("Hardness" was brewer's jargon for "sourness," but Dickens seems to have meant that it was a strong ale, brewed with hard water.) The best Scotch ale, like that taken by the Bagman's uncle, was cloyingly sweet and sometimes so glutinous that it was reputed to stick your hand shut in five minutes. After bottling, such ale was left five years in a cool, dry cellar, and then four months near a Dutch oven in frequent use; thus matured, it was drunk almost as a liqueur. *Dombey*'s little Mr. Perch of Ball's Pond likes it with his cutlet.

But industrialism gradually drove out many such local brews, while in their places rose the modern giants, most of which were already established: Whitbread (1742), Worthington (1744), Guinness (1759), Bass (1777), Ind Coope

### COUNTRY INN SCENE

Ale-post, inn-sign, quart pot, and two "regulars" compose a scene that is still re-enacted many times every day in England. The paraphernalia of the hanging inn-sign can be traced back to Roman times, when an evergreen bush or a broom was hung out to indicate an ale-house. During the 1700s inn-signs became so elaborate that they sometimes formed an arch over the roadway, and legislation had to be enacted limiting their size.

and the rest. Their standardized products were sold at an increasing number of "tied houses," taverns owned or financed by the brewer.

Because of the suitability for brewing of the water from the river Trent, Burton-on-Trent became the site of several breweries whose bottled products were commonly found in London, once the railroad made national distribution possible. Indeed, the freight vaults under St. Pancras Station were built using the dimensions of a barrel of Burton ale as the modular unit. But the most popular malt drink there was brewed with good tawny Thames water in the city itself: porter. This was supposedly developed about 1722 by Ralph Harwood of the Bell Brewhouse, Shoreditch, in imitation of a mixture of three ales commonly called for in taverns by porters or navvies, "three-threads" or "thirds." Brewers called his time-saver "entire," but the name "porter" was quickly applied to it, some think, because porters were so fond of it. It ran a percent or so higher in alcohol than ale and was darker and sweeter, more malty and less hopped, but not so dark or rich as stout. For a variety of reasons chemical and technical, porter became the perfect subject for one of the earliest experiments in the mass production of foodstuffs, as well as in mass promotion. As an instance of the "puffing" of porter, one brewer put about an image of Brittania with the patriotic subscription, "Pray Sup-Port Her"; for before 1836 the beer-tax was a source of much revenue to the Crown.

Southwark was "the Town of Malt," as Dickens' friend Blanchard Jerrold called it, and its immense workings were the pride of Londoners and an important feature of Dickens' "essential London":

> The massive drays are out; the prodigious draymen are arrayed in their leather . . . the stately horses that are . . . the pride of the English brewer are tossing their noble heads and pawing the ground. The barrels are rolling and swinging in all directions. . . . Before the ordinary tradesman has touched his shutters, lumbering processions of heavily laden drays are debouching on various quarters of London, bearing the famous "entire" to scores of customers.

Each brewery maintained a stable of Belgian workhorses, as many as two hundred, worth, they said, £80 each. Their harness bore the brewer's sign: an anchor for Barclay, a horseshoe for Meux, an hour-glass for Calvert.

At "a choice old wainscoted public house near Scotland Yard," Dickens found coal-heavers "quaffing Barclay's Best"—as well he might, for Barclay

## THE BARMAID

By 1849, the date of this illustration, the bar was already evolving into its present island or peninsula from its earlier glassed-in cage, and pub patrons were both served and drank at the bar. Taking a leaf from gin-palaces, publicans were installing pretty young women to serve out the drinks and entertain the customers. The characteristic Victorian beer engine, with its row of pulls connected by pipes to beer-barrels in the cellar, had already made its appearance.

and the next largest porter–house, Truman, were sending forth 50,000 gallons a day for London alone. No wonder Lady Tippins (OMF) thinks navvies "drink porter out of their barrows"! At the Barclay brewery, steam engines found an early use in pumping water from the river into elevated cisterns, and in running the "Jacob's ladder" or conveyor belt that carried malt upward to dim heights within the vast brewhouse. Below was an earthen floor, where the brewery in its growth had swallowed a graveyard, which stood desolate in the midst of one hundred and fifty gargantuan store–vats, each holding about 30,000 gallons of porter worth some £300,000. The smoke from the brewing was carried off by towering brick chimneys, which were London landmarks. It blackened everything, etched fantastic patterns on windows, and kept some flowers, such as the yellow rose, from growing within ten miles of the town.

As Pip learns, it was a "crack thing" to brew; the Havisham fortune in that novel comes from brewing, while in Thackeray's *Pendennis*, Henry Foker inherits his father's brewery, makers of "Foker's Entire," and an income from it of at least £14,000 a year. In 1823 the brewer Meux (pronounced "Mews") gave a party in one of his enormous new vats, no doubt to celebrate the fact that he had tripled his already large fortune in a few years of brewing porter. By 1836 there were twelve principal London breweries, which brewed in that year over two million barrels of malt beverages; the London population then stood at about 1,500,000.

Poverty and "heavy wet" were friends, too, as were poverty and oysters according to Sam Weller, for porter was cheap enough at three or four pence a pint. Life in debtors' prisons was "all porter and skittles," Sam said, for there were no creditors to interrupt the tap–room and skittle–alley existence that had brought many of the inmates there in the first place. Mr. Pickwick bequeaths 25 gallons of porter to the denizens of the Fleet when he leaves, while Mr. Micawber in the King's Bench Prison begs the price of four pints of porter from David Copperfield, and pays him immediately with a little lecture on the evils of borrowing. A clerk dining often had porter, as Pip and Herbert Pocket do at a "geographical chop–house" where there are maps of the world in porter–pot rims all over the table–cloths. Shrimps and porter were popular, too (Susan Nipper in *Dombey* likes them), and Kit Nubbles treats to oysters and beer after the show at Astley's Circus (OCS). Enormous porter–cans were sometimes used as comic theater props, while the real thing, only a little smaller, would be circulating among the audience. For Noah Claypole (OT) oysters and porter suffice, but burglar Bill Sikes selects porter and sheeps' heads, which is Dickens' way of having his bit of fun, for the latter were called "jemmies," like

" HEAVY WET."

King William and Reform, I say,
    In such a case who can be neuter?
Just let me blow the froth away,
    And see how I will drain the pewter

Another tankard, landlord, fill,
    And let us drink to that ere chap, Broom;
And then we'll chaunt God save King Bill,
    And send the echoes thro' the tap-room.

"Heavy Wet," or porter, was the workingman's beverage, and was inevitably linked to porters, one of whom is shown here blowing the head off his pint. The accompanying verse attests to the popularity of the reduction of the duty on beer and other reforms enacted during the reign of William IV. Not the least of these was the loosening of legal restrictions on the licensing of ale-houses as part of a government campaign to combat gin consumption. By 1834 there were over 20,000 in England.

his tools. Thackeray has provided a diagram of a typical middle class table–setting:

| Porter pot | Potatoes | Quart of ale |
|---|---|---|
| Roast leg of pork, with sage and onions | Three shreds of celery in a glass | Broiled haddock, removed by Hashed Mutton |
| Porter pot | Cabbage | Fine old Golden Sherry |

For a boating trip up the Thames, Fortnum and Mason might put up a box of cold mutton sandwiches, captain's biscuits, and a bottle or two of mild porter.

Pot–boys (or potmen) delivered porter from the ale–house to private dwellings: thus Dick Swiveller (OCS) salutes his first day on the job in Sampson Brass's law office by commanding a pot of mild porter from a passing "beer–boy," which he pays for instantly to establish his credit. The pot–boy would have been a valuable ally, lugging "many a supper–pint well–frothed" through the teeming courts of slum areas, and returning the empty pewter pots to the public–house, his head full of local gossip and with the newspapers under his arm:

> . . . the nine o'clock "beer" comes round with a lantern in front of his tray, and says, as he lends Mr. Walker "Yesterday's 'Tiser," that he's blest if he can hardly hold the pot, much less feel the paper, for it's one of the bitterest nights he ever felt, 'cept the night when the man was frozen to death in the brickfield.

Later he may "employ himself for the remainder of the evening in assiduously stirring the tap–room fire, and deferentially taking part in the conversation of the worthies assembled around it," occasionally being called upon, as we have seen earlier, to make "burnt Sherry" or Flip or to eject an obstreperous drunk.

In *Nickleby* we learn that slum doorways were always "blocked up by a motley collection of children and porter–pots of all sizes, from the babe in arms and the half–pint pot, to the full–grown girl and the half–gallon can." And on a fine morning the railings outside a popular pub like the Princess's Arms (DS) were hung with pewter, an easy mark for a thief. In 1820 the publicans of London claimed that they were losing £100,000 a year to "cat and kitten hunters" who stole quart and pint pots. Noah Claypole in *Oliver* proudly presents three kittens and a cat to Fagin, who is duly scornful; for this sort of "sneaksmanship" was low, on a level with "bug–hunting" (rolling drunks), whereas Fagin's boys are expert pickpockets, "stookbuzzers" (handkerchiefs) and "tailbuzzers of dummies and skins" (purses and wallets). They "nail props" (pins and brooches) and "wire sneezers" (snuff-boxes). Bill Sikes himself is a "cracksman" or "rampsman," and hence one of the elite of Newgate.

Our taste for porter has led us into bad company, and we begin to see why "black porter" was not usually favored by the gentry, who likened it to "the eloquence of Mirabeau, froth at the top, heavy and muddy within." In its murky depths, it was charged, there was liquorice, vitriol, cocculus indicus, even horse–meat. No such charge was ever proved, and it is likely that Victorian porter was as safe to drink as anything else then, and a good deal safer than water. Its black color came from honest roasted malt, called caramel. So long as pewter pots were common, only esthetes objected to the color of an ale, but in 1845 the excise–tax on glass was repealed, and many landlords bought glass tankards, in which "sparkling bright" ale appealed to the eye as well as to the taste. The ales of Burton–on–Trent, such as Allsopp's, mentioned in "Somebody's Luggage," swiftly grew in favor. From 1863, when porter's share of the London market was 75%, it slowly lost ground to mild and bitter ale until in 1899 porter's share was only one–quarter.

The increasing popularity of Guinness' Dublin stout, and London varieties such as Reid's Celebrated, further deepened the twilight of porter brewers, many of which failed to "diversify" or to merge with brewers of other draughts. Stout tastes strongly of both malt and hops, and like porter takes its dark color from caramel. It runs about 6.0% alcohol, while "double–stout" may have been stronger (although there may have been a confusion, perhaps deliberate, between "Dublin" and "double"). Its popularity is shown by the placard displayed at The Magpie and Stump tavern (PWP), claiming that its cellars contain "500,000 barrels of double–stout," giving rise to the question "as to where in the bowels of the earth this mighty cellar might be supposed to exist." One recalls also that hypochondriacal widow of the *Sketches*, Mrs. Bloss, who keeps a large hamper full of bottles of Guinness and washes her pills down with it.

As a young man, Dickens had heard the chimes of the Coalhole and Evans's "Cave of Harmony," where double and even triple stout were offered, and he may well have been found "flaring away like winkin'—going to the theater— supping at harmonic meetings—eating oysters by the barrel—drinking stout by the gallon—even stopping out all night, and coming home as cool in the morning as if nothing had happened," like "young White" and the aforementioned Potter and Smithers. Oyster–houses often sold stout, and also ginger–beer, some as strong as beer, most mere soda–pop; the placards for it depicted "customers submerged in the effervescence, or stunned by flying corks." It must have been very gingery, for M. Taine, who sampled it at Cremorne Gardens, said it tasted like lemonade "with peppers and pimientos . . . it set your mouth on fire." Mixed with ale, it became "Shandygaff." The Magpie and Stump tavern, again, also sold "Dantzic Spruce," a sort of beer made with fermented spruce twigs and ginger, and "Devonshire Cider,"

The Ale House

At about the mid-point of Victoria's reign, English consumption of malt beverages reached an annual rate of about a barrel a head, compared to less than half that figure to-day, and the ale-house was the principal place of resort of the man in the street. Convivial evenings in company were the order of the day, but other entertainments included cock fights, pit-bulldog contests, and rat-catching terriers.

considered to be the best going; but the so-called "Cyder Cellers," frequented as a supper–rooms by the crowd from the Adelphi Theater next door, served mostly stout and brandy.

"Small beer," "table–beer," or "swipes," was a weak beer often served free with meals, and in consequence held in contempt by he–men. An inscription on a tombstone in the cathedral close at Winchester speaks to this matter in an exemplary sentence:

> Here sleeps in peace a Hampshire Grenadier,
> Who caught his death by drinking cold small beer.

Soldiers be wise from his untimely fall,
And when you're hot drink Strong or none at all.

Small beer's non–alcoholic cousin, toast–and–water, was made by soaking toast in warm water overnight. It is given to his pupils by Squeers in *Nickleby*, sweetened with a tot of spirits; and Dickens sometimes drank it instead of wine on the banquet–circuit, a trick he got from actors who used toast–and–water as a stage–wine. At one of Dickens' clubs, the Athenaeum, however, when "toast–and–water" was called for by celebrants in "The Temperance Corner," waiters knowingly translated it into something stronger.

The last reference to drink in Dickens' work is to ale, taken by Dick Datchery with a simple supper in *Drood*. This serves to remind us that, though other drinks may have their little day in England, ale will probably have the last word—or is it the last sip?

The Englishman's willingness to try anything has led over the centuries to a host of combinations of malt beverages, a small sampling of which we append here: *Shandygaff*, often drunk on excursions "up the river," combines equal portions of ale and ginger beer or ginger ale, to which a little lemon juice and ginger brandy may be profitably added. Made with lemonade and pale ale it becomes a *Small–Lem–and–a–Dash*, "the poor man's Champagne," and with Scotch ale a *"Wait-a-Bit."* Half old ale and half bitter ale was known, inevitably, as a *Mother-in-Law*, while *Uncle*, for the same reason, united old ale and mild ale. *Cooper* consists of Dublin stout and London porter, a "capitol" drink to our pun–loving grandsires; and an equal mixture of stout and bitter ale was called a *John Bright* after the Victorian reform politician. *Arf-and-Arf* to a London tippler was half porter and half ale, but to his New York counterpart it mingled old ale and new. Poured together into a pilsener glass, equal parts of Guinness stout and Champagne make a *Black Velvet*, the favorite tipple of Bismarck. Evelyn Waugh devotes an amusing scene in *Put Out More Flags* to "Blackers" as it was then called. Crab the Apothecary in Smollett's *Roderick Random* drinks a potation called *Pop–In*, compounded of a quartern of brandy and a quart of small beer.

|  |  |
|---|---|
| *Buttered Ale* | Allow a quarter-pound of unsalted butter to warm to room temperature. Heat a pint of ale to blood temperature and pour it over the butter. Beat to a smooth consistency and serve warm (but not hot) in tankards. |
| *Hot Spiced Ale* | *1 qt. good ale; 1/2 grated nutmeg; 2 eggs well beaten; 1 piece unsalted butter; 1 piece dry toast.* |
|  | Heat (but do not boil) the ale, then add nutmeg. Mix beaten eggs with a little cold ale. Add the hot ale to the egg mixture and keep stirring until it froths. Add a piece of butter and float the dry toast on top. Serve in tankards. |
| *'Tween-Decks Cup or Splitting Headache* | *1/4 pt. rum; 2 qts. ale; 6 cloves, crushed; a little cinnamon, ginger, and nutmeg, grated.* |

Put the spices into the rum to steep for an hour, then strain.
Add the ale and mix well.

### Cambridge Ale Cup

*1 oz. each of cloves, mace, and cinnamon; grated nutmeg; 3
oz. powdered sugar; juice and peel of 1 lemon; 3 pts. ale;
1/2 pt. Sherry; thin strips of dry toast.*

Bruise the spices and boil them for an hour in three pints of
water, then strain and add the rest of the ingredients. Serve
hot, with a strip of toast and grated nutmeg on top, in goblets or tankards.

### Cool Tankard

*1 qt. mild ale; 1 glass white wine; 1 glass brandy; grated
nutmeg; dry toast; 1 glass capillaire; juice of 1 lemon; 1 roll
of lemon peel; sprig of borage or lemon balm or slice of
cucumber rind.*

Combine all the ingredients. Serve with nutmeg grated on
top, a sprig of herbs, and a bit of toast.

*A Note on Toast*: We trust that our American readers understand by the term "toast" a piece of bread that has been
browned before a fire or under a grill unit on a stove, and not
that soft square that comes out of an electrical device.

# Chapter Nine

# "*Wine, Ma'am, Wine*"
### JINGLE

"I know a good 'ouse where we can have a red hot chop for dinner, and a glass of good wine," wrote Dickens to his friend John Forster. When not overwhelmed with work he loved "a long walk with a good dinner at the end of it," and a fireside chat over a bottle of wine in congenial company. In this yearning mood, Dick Swiveller speaks glowingly of "rosy wine," even though his glass holds only cold gin-and-water: " 'Fan the sinking flame of hilarity with the wing of friendship; and pass the rosy. . . . ' "

Chesterton spoke of Dickens' "poetry of comfort," his ability to create a mood of cosiness, "of two friends drinking wine together and talking through an endless night and pouring wine from an inexhaustible bottle." This is just the sort of comfort which Martin Chuzzlewit and his friends find at the White Hart Inn, Salisbury, after a long, cold, windy walk over the Wiltshire Downs:

> A famous Inn! the hall of a very grove of dead game, and dangling joints of mutton . . . an illustrious larder, with glass doors, developing cold fowls and noble joints, and tarts wherein the raspberry jam coyly withdrew itself . . . behind a lattice–work of pastry. . . . a fire piled half–way up the chimney, plates warming before it, wax–candles gleaming everywhere, and a table spread for three, with silver and glass enough for thirty . . . .
>
> . . . nobody ever dreamed such soup as was put upon the table . . . or such fish; or such side–dishes; or such a top and bottom; or such a course of birds and sweets; or in short anything approaching the reality of that entertainment at ten-and-sixpence a head, exclusive of wines. As to *them*, the man who can dream such iced champagne, such claret, port, or sherry, had better go to bed and stop there.

John Westlock plays host on this occasion, and a good and generous one he is:

Nor had he the least objection to laugh at himself, as he demonstrated

My Dear Forster.

You don't feel disposed, do you. to muffle yourself up, and start off with me for a good brisk walk over Hampstead Heath? I know a good 'uns there where we can have a red hot chop for dinner, and a glass of good wine.

All work and no play makes Jack a dull boy. I am as dull as a codfish.

Faithfully Thine CD.

If you can, say "yes" & I'll come down

## AN INVITATION FROM DICKENS

Dickens' was a restless soul, and his mountainous correspondence is filled with hastily scrawled notes such as this to his closest friend and *confidant*, John Forster, inviting him on an evening tramp over Hampstead Heath, to be followed by a "red hot chop" and some "good wine" at a "good 'ouse"—either "Jack Straw's Castle" or "The Spaniard's."

when . . . the head–waiter inquired with respectful solicitude whether that port, being a light and tawny wine, was suited to his taste, or whether he would wish to try a fruity port with greater body. To this John gravely answered that he was well satisfied with what he had, which he esteemed, as one might say, a pretty tidy vintage: for which the waiter thanked him and withdrew. And then John told his friends, with a broad grin, that he supposed it was all right, but he didn't know; and went off into a perfect shout.

They were very merry and full of enjoyment the whole time, but not the least pleasant part of the festival was when they all three sat about the fire, cracking nuts, drinking wine, and talking cheerfully.

As this is indeed the poetry of comfortable sociability, that very Victorian observance, the Public Dinner, must be its prose: "waiters, with wine-baskets in their hands, place decanters of sherry down the tables at very respectable distances," the whiskered guests assemble, turbot, poultry, lobster sauce, and jellies vanish like lightning, "hearty eaters wipe their foreheads, and . . . ask you to take wine in the most friendly way possible." The hum of conversation is general and loud—and now the Toastmaster stands, praying silence:

"Gentlemen, charge your glasses, if you please!" Decanters having been handed about, and glasses filled, the toastmaster proceeds, in a regular ascending scale:—"Gentlemen—air—you—all—charged? Pray—silence—gentlemen—for—the—cha—i—r!" (*Boz*)

The Chairman rises, says he will be brief, is not—but receives an ovation anyway, probably on account of his finishing at all. "God Save the Queen" is sung by professional gentlemen, and the evening goes off with a great clinking of glasses—and shillings, for it is a Charity Dinner. The very grandest of such dinners ran to sixty–odd dishes, eaten under looming frosted-silver epergnes laden with hot-house fruit. They included ices and wafers; tea; French, Iberian and Rhine wines; liquers and cordials; and Roman Punch.

The banquet after the Muggleton-Dingley Dell cricket match in *Pickwick* is more vivacious: Mr. Jingle's capabilities as a toastmaster, like Dickens' own, emerge quickly, even though he is a perfect stranger to most of the company; and he sings a song in which the words " 'bowl' 'sparkling' 'ruby' 'bright' and 'wine' " are frequently repeated at short intervals. When they get home afterwards the Pickwickians have obviously been "dining." Mr. Pickwick's hat is permanently cocked over one eye and he smiles incessantly at nothing at all, while Snodgrass is sunk in a poet's "abject and hopeless misery":

"Is anything the matter with Mr. Snodgrass, sir?" inquired Emily, with great anxiety.

"Nothing the matter, ma'am," replied [Jingle], "Cricket dinner—glorious party—capital songs—old port—claret—good—very good—wine, ma'am—wine."

"It wasn't the wine," murmured Mr. Snodgrass, in a broken voice. "It was the salmon." (Somehow or other, it never *is* the wine in these cases.)

Wine drinking at table was not simply an accompaniment to food but was part of the ceremonial of dining, for guests regularly invited each other to "take wine" with them, glasses were raised and drained, and nods of acknowledgement exchanged, as we see Watkins Tottle and Miss Lillerton doing in an early sketch. Then there was the custom of toasting, the word perhaps derived from the piece of toast put in medieval wine drinks to serve as a filter. However that may be, toasting, in the sweet Sherry (called "Bristol Milk") and claret that were drunk with meals in early-Victorian times, began while the ladies were still present. But they soon withdrew, the cloth was drawn, and a dish of walnuts and decanters of port were placed upon the mahogany. While the ladies sipped currant wine or Curaçao upstairs, a convivial host of the old school would "challenge everybody to drink wine," as Thackeray says, "bobbing to one man, and winking to another, and tossing his glass" as he sang a song, or solemnly addressing his guests "with his wine-glass on his bosom." The Queen, the Church, the Army and Navy ("Hearts of Oak and Oaken Ships!"), and the professions, were all toasted—and of course "The Ladies!," who might be heard overhead "dancing the Spanish dance among themselves." When the gentlemen who were still ambulant rejoined the ladies in the drawing-room, "young men who were too bashful to dance before supper, found tongues and partners," while their elders took flirtatious "furniture walks" with each others' wives. A Negus might be served, or a bowl of punch. But some men never made it to the drawing-room, and remained snoring in their dining chairs until tall footmen, plushclad, with bulging (perhaps artificial) calves, loosened their stocks and ties, and carried them chair and all to their cabs and carriages.

It had been a Georgian custom to drink a bottle at least of fortified wine after dinner; William IV expected his ministers to be two-bottle men, if only to keep level with the typical Anglican cleric in a country living. Under Victoria such excesses moderated, but the Pickwickians have the older habit, and linger over their Port at The Bull Inn, Rochester, where the child Dickens may well have seen such gentlemen at their "sitting." Mr. Jingle makes very free with Mr.

Pickwick's wine: " 'bottle stands—pass it round—way of the sun—through the buttonhole—no heeltaps,' and he emptied his glass, which he had filled about two minutes before . . . with the air of a man who was used to it." Port was always passed clockwise, "the way of the sun," and a man who emptied his bottle was said to have "buzzed" it.

> [A little later] Mr. Tupman looked round him. The wine, which had exerted its somniferous influence over Mr. Snodgrass and Mr. Winkle, had stolen upon the senses of Mr. Pickwick. That gentleman had gradually . . . undergone the ordinary transitions from the height of conviviality to the depth of misery, and from the depth of misery to the height of conviviality. Like a gas-lamp in the street, with the wind in the pipe, he had exhibited for a moment an unnatural brilliancy: then sunk so low as to be scarcely discernible: after a short interval, he had burst out again, to enlighten for a moment, then flickered with an uncertain, staggering sort of light, and then gone out altogether.

Not to put too fine a point on it, he is "elephants." Mr. Pickwick must have been born about 1760, when Port was Port; even as late as a hundred years later, however, four-fifths of all the wine drunk in England was still of the fortified sort. The popularity of Port dates from the Treaty of Methuen in 1703, which imposed a heavy tariff on French wine while encouraging Iberian imports for political reasons. Then, too, the wines of Spain and Portugal were easy to import by sea, whereas many French and German wines did not become readily available until the continental rail system developed. Consequently claret, Burgundy, Champagne, brandy and hock were imported—sometimes smuggled in—at a price, and were therefore traditionally associated with aristocracy, Toryism, and secret allegiance to the Lost Cause of the deposed and exiled Stuart pretenders to the throne. On the other hand, a taste for Port, Sherry, or rum suggested Whig principles, adherence to the Constitution, and the solid virtues of merchant, squire, and the professions.

The aristocrat of Iberian wines was "vintage Port," the wine of a certain excellent year. Dickens had 1834 port (at £35 a dozen in 1850) in his cellar at his death, some of which he had offered to a friend, saying "I have kept a few lingering caskets with a genie enshrined within, expressly for you." Port of the same era seemed the right wine for an especially "moist and vinous" clergyman in the *Sketches*, who also likes "comet vintages." Comets were supposedly signs of good wine years, such as Halley's in 1834 and the Great Comet of 1843. Biela's obliging comet appeared every six and a half years from 1772 to 1846, when it split up and vanished. Vintners and other scientists were still looking for it in 1872 when it appeared for the last time in the spectacular form of 100 meteors a minute over Europe, to the open-mouthed delight of wine-lovers. The vintages seem to have been unremarkable, however. The stars on brandy bottles today reflect a residual influence of this superstition, suggesting that each of the vintages blended into the final liquor came from a comet year.

"Crusted Port" was often merely an ordinary Port bottled early so that it formed a "crust" of impurities. Since this was wrongly thought to be a sign of quality in Port, some wine–sellers roughened the insides of their bottles by shaking buckshot in them to encourage the wine to throw down a crust. This may be what Pickwick's landlady Mrs. Bardell has in her parlor closet: "crusted port—that at one and nine"—far too cheap to be the genuine article.

Sherry was said to have come into fashion when the Prince Regent tired of Madeira and announced that he would drink nothing but Sherry, and it has been coming in and going out ever since. Victorians long preferred "Old Brown," a Sherry of the oloroso type. It was much easier to make cheaply or to counterfeit than the pale dry fino Sherries, which became fashionable later in the century; Mr. Sapsea (ED) talks about pale Sherry, but quite typically he is drinking Port at the time.

Decanters of sweet Sherry were available in hotel dining-rooms as a matter of course, full of crumbs, smells and fatigue; so that old India hand, Major Jos. Bagstock (DS), takes his own East India Brown Sherry along when he travels, in a pocket flask. This was a fine brown Sherry that had been shipped from Spain to India (sometimes to the West Indies), warehoused for a time, and brought back to England improved by the heat and sea–motion. Mrs. Bardell in *Pickwick* has a bottle of "the celebrated East-India Sherry at 14–pence;" but since the real thing cost about eight shillings a bottle, Mrs. Bardell can have little more than spiked elderberry wine, probably brought in from Germany and driven slowly past the India Dock in the vintner's dray.

No other wine was so much carried about in pocket flasks. Lawyer Jaggers in *Great Expectations* takes Sherry from a flask with a sandwich for a hasty lunch in chambers, while portable Sherry appears in Trollope's novels whenever his characters fall off their horses. At hunt breakfasts after 1850 "six dozen of really good sherry . . . have been known to establish the reputation of a new resident . . . ," while the ordinary breakfast at a gentleman's shooting-box included cutlets and Curaçao, with ale and perhaps claret-and-water. Mulled claret and Danish cherry brandy were served as stirrup cups; and everyone filled a flask before setting out, for a dram had replaced bleeding as the treat-

## BUMBLE AND MRS. CORNEY

This could be an illustration of the two workhouse employees drinking a restorative peppermint gin out of a tea-cup; but instead the beverage really is tea, being taken after sharing a bottle of "native Port." Thus inflamed, Bumble proposes marriage to the formidable matron, is accepted, and soon becomes the long-suffering spouse of a virago.

ment for the jolts of the field—some of which were caused by too many jolts at breakfast. The hunt-club members wore boots dyed mahogany with Port-wine and blackberry jam, or pink with apricot jam and Champagne.

Madeira was as strong and as popular as Port and Sherry—"the malvoisie of the Isle of Madeer in Portyngale," malmsey, or "Maideary" as some Victorians said. Madeira and Champagne are both served at the luncheon of the directors of the fraudulent Anglo-Bengalee Company, in *Martin Chuzzlewit*, a scene memorable for the presence of Mr. Jobling, whose unctuous voice is like "light shining through the ruddy medium of choice old Burgundy."

The country–made "reds and whites" (red currant or raspberry, white currant or cowslip wines) were sweetly delicious but of lowly social status. Thackeray in *The Newcomes* dismisses a country family with " 'Two balls in the season, and ten dozen of gooseberry, are good enough for *them*.' " The best South African wine, Constantia, was frequently brought out from ladies' parlor closets with a plate of sweet Palmers biscuits when daytime callers came. It is given to Reverend Mr. Crisparkle (ED) when his mother thinks he needs picking up. Mr. Wilding, the wine–merchant of "No Thorofare," enjoys a biscuit and a glass of forty–five–year–old Port "from the best corner of the binn of that year," a combination actually called a "wine–merchant's tea."

Such wine as Mr. Wilding's was sold in quiet London offices over extensive vaults, candle-lit and rumorous of the traffic overhead; and a bottle of his old Port might cost as much as a clerk would earn in a week. Most Victorian wine, of course, had no such pedigree. Kidd's *Iniquities of London* (1844) wildly claimed that two-thirds of all the Port sold in London was made there: "dozens of bumper toasts . . . gulped down in *native port*! Bottled Yesterday! and still shaking from the hamper!" So Mr. Bumble (OT) praises the Port he brings to Mrs. Corney as " 'real, fresh, genuine . . . only out of the cask this forenoon; clear as a bell and no sediment.' " The adulteration of Port began on the Douro itself, where elderberries and cherries were sometimes added to the must as well as brandy. The Duke of Wellington claimed to have been served a bottle of Port with a dead rat in it. "A small rat, Sir," brightly suggested a subaltern. "It was a damned big rat, Sir!" retorted the Duke. "A very large bottle, then," tried the hapless subaltern—only to be blown up with "Damme, I tell you, it was a damned *small* bottle!" Cynics said that Port required three good vintages: one of grapes, one of brandy, and one of elderberries.

In *The Uncommercial Traveller* Dickens speaks with seasoned bitterness of such wines as "the old–established Bull's Head fruity port; whose reputation was gained solely by the old–established price the Bull's Head put upon it."

## SHARING A COBBLER

One of the New World's most popular gifts to the Old was the Cobbler, a sweetened wine drink served on ice, that got its name from a Hudson River Valley Dutch dialect word for a heap of rocks, represented by chunks of ice. The ice probably came from New England ponds. English visitors to the United States in the 1830s and 1840s, like Dickens, popularized the taste for Cobblers, which because they were drunk through straws were much favored by romantic young couples. The couple above are at "The Casino," in Holborn, one of the new dancing salons that became popular about the same time.

Waiters called this sort of wine "strap," while better wine was "rum gutlers." The Eagle Hotel in Straffordshire, which Dickens thought he had better call the "Dodo," had Sherry so bad that he wrote:

> If I were to send my pint of wine to some famous chemist to be analyzed, what would it turn out to be made of? It tastes of pepper, sugar, bitter almonds, vinegar, warm knives, any flat drink, and a little brandy. Would it unman a Spanish exile by reminding him of his native land at all? I think not.

It might have made a German homesick, though, for the notorious "Hambro sherries"—as surely this was—were made on the Elbe.

There were also uncertain French wines. The Veneering's butler, "a gloomy analytical chemist," seems always to be saying, after " 'Chablis, sir?'—'you wouldn't if you knew what it's made of' " (OMF). Claret (from "clarrie," an herb used to flavor red wines in the Middle Ages) is said to have been sometimes spiked with brandy before shipment to England to make it travel better, but also because English taste was dragooned by Port. In 1837 Stendhal visited a "wine–manufactory" in Marseilles, where "with wine, sugar, iron–filings, and certain floral essences they made the wines of all countries." You could order 150 hogsheads of any wines you liked in the morning and take delivery in the afternoon. In England, manuals for hotel-managers like that of "Bacchus" suggested that a new fruity wine with plenty of brandy fretted in and a little cream of tartar to give it a certain hardness is the kind of drink the "uneducated palate would appreciate."

A "new man" might fill his newly carpentered bins with such inferior wine, and pass it off to his newly made friends as having been "ages" in his cellar—a claim belied by the smell of fresh mortar that came up on the bottles. Surtees lists the contents of such a cellar in his hunting-farce, *Mr. Sponge's Sporting Tour* (1853):

> Two dozen of pale sherry at 26s., and one dozen brown ditto at 48s.; three bottles of Bucellas, of "the finest quality imported" at 38s. a doz.; Lisbon "rich and dry," at 32s., and some marvelous creaming champagne at 48s. . . . first–growth Chateaux Margaux "Wintle," at 66s. in very rich-ly–cut decanters . . . old 36s. port.

Lisbon was a "familiar name in City wine rooms" to Dickens as a young man, and probably Bucellas as well. Both were drunk unbrandied by the Portuguese, who never liked any of the spiked wines they shipped to England.

All the fortified wines faded in popularity in late Victorian times, while French and German wines flourished. Gladstone's budget of 1860 lowered the tariffs on French wine, many varieties of which, together with the Rhines and Mosels, were becoming available for the first time in England, in part encouraged by new laws permitting grocers to stock and sell wine. This was a boon to the rising middle-class, for there had never been enough vintage Port, or decent, inexpensive wines of any sort, for that matter, to go around. London's better clubs developed excellent cellars, although there were few public places as good as the Gray's Inn Coffee House, with its "rows of decanters, burly as if with the consciousness of pipes of expensive port wine below" in its famed vaults. Gentlemen's sons might even be unofficially instructed in vintage–lore at school by the college wine steward or an indulgent mentor.

Dickens stocked his cellar with Brâne-Mouton (now Mouton–Rothschild), a superb claret, and Chambertin, Clos de Vougeot and Volnay Burgundies. His Rhines were Schloss Johannisberger and Zeltingen Schlossberg, both superior. An admirer had once sent him a bottle of sparkling Moselle as a gift, and he wrote gratefully that he would drink it while writing the next number of *Oliver Twist*, which was to be "light." The sparkle of wine is indeed embodied in that delightful scene involving Mr. Bumble, Mrs. Corney, and a bottle of peppermint gin we treated above. Queen Victoria stimulated the popularity of Rhenish wine by the repute of her cellar, by her visit to the Rhine vineyards, and, according to one source, by a verse she liked to recite: "A little drop of hock / Keeps away the doc." It is so incredible that it may be true.

Hock, claret, Champagne—nearly any wine—were often made into "wine cups," cool summer drinks with citrus fruits, sugar and herbal flavorings. They were often served in the silver loving cups considered so appropriate as gifts by Dickens and his circle. After a public reading in Boston in 1868, Dickens and a party that included the poet Longfellow were entertained at the home of James and Annie Fields in Charles Street, where Dickens made a cup for the company, for his reputation as a compounder had preceded him. In it, he said, was a little Sherry, some brandy, some cider and "lemon, of course. I put lemons in all my punches. But nobody has hit upon that elusive ingredient that makes a world of difference . . . it's a European herb used in France for its soothing properties. You'll find it sometimes in French salads." Someone guessed catnip, but the answer was borage, an herb with a flavor like cucumber. Dickens jotted down his recipe for "Cider Cup" for the Fields, and also for his Champagne, Claret and Moselle Cups.

But iced Champagne was the coming thing. As one authority remarks, "the age was becoming democratic, and Champagne, with all its gas and glitter, is pre–eminently the wine of democracy." Martin Chuzzlewit had found it so on his visit, years ago, to America. For the servants at Dombey's wedding-banquet, "champagne has grown too common among them to be mentioned, and everyone is in such high spirits that the cook proposes . . . that they all go in a party to the play." But one footman is staring at things without seeing them, being overcome, as he says, with the "exciseman" of the occasion, while another "appears to have his head glued to the table. . . . "

In spite of his own man–of–the–world pleasure in fine wine, references to it in Dickens' later novels take on a grave or satiric tone quite different from the old warmth and conviviality. Iced Champagne is a forcible image of the chilling of Dombey's human affections. At the christening of little Paul Dombey there is a cold collation "set forth in a cold pomp of glass and silver . . . like a dead dinner lying in state. . . . "

> "Mr. John," said Mr. Dombey, "will you take the bottom of the table, if you please. What have you got there, Mr. John?"
>
> "I have got a cold fillet of veal here, sir," replied Mr. Chick, rubbing his numbed hands together. "What have *you* got there, sir?"
>
> "This," returned Mr. Dombey, "is some cold preparation of calf's head, I think. I see cold fowls—ham—patties—salad—lobster. Miss Tox will do me the honour of taking some wine? Champagne to Miss Tox."
>
> There was a toothache in everything. The wine was so bitter cold that it forced a little scream from Miss Tox. . . .

At Dombey's loveless wedding, Dickens forces us to examine the remains of the banquet: "crumbs, dirty plates, spillings of wine, half-thawed ice, stale discoloured heel–taps, scraps of lobster, drum–sticks of fowls, and pensive jellies, gradually resolving themselves into a lukewarm gummy soup." But Dickens himself laid down just the sort of Champagne Dombey might have served: Bouzy, a first–growth wine in the classification of 1855.

As a contrast to Mr. Dombey, Dickens gives us gentle old Sol Gills, who cherishes a last bottle of fine old Madeira in his cellar as a talisman for the safe return of his beloved nephew, Walter Gay, from Barbados. Victorian readers knew without being told that Madeira was never drunk chilled, that it was the antithesis of Dombey's cold wine. They knew too that fine Madeira was often "double–voyaged," having travelled safely to the West Indies and back to mellow it. They might even have remembered, as surely Dickens did, the famous pipe of Madeira that had been sunk in a shipwreck in 1778, and was brought up in 1814 a superb wine. Walter does survive a shipwreck, and Gill's wine is finally drunk in grateful celebration of his miraculous return from death at sea, and also of the return from death–in–life by Mr. Dombey himself, redeemed by suffering.

> A bottle that has long been excluded from the light of day, and is hoary with dust and cobwebs, has been brought into the sunshine, and the golden wine within it sheds a lustre on the table. It is the last bottle of the old madeira.

Another aspect of wine that increasingly compelled Dickens' imagination was that of wine stored for years in dark vaults, as in a tomb or prison—an image of buried life. Real prisons had always obsessed Dickens; now psychological imprisonment became a preoccupation as well. Deep–rooted alcoholic deterioration born of sorrow and loneliness, and encouraged for his own purposes by Uriah Heep, is almost clinically depicted in Mr. Wickfield of *David Copperfield*, who sits brooding over his Port night after night. And David Copperfield's deadly, puritanically tainted step–father, Edward Murdstone, tries to bottle up David's childhood emotions just as he might bottle the wine in his vaults, for his is a partner in Murdstone and Grimsby, wine-merchants. In *Little Dorrit*, society, which maintains prisons like the Marshalsea, is itself no less a prison, where fine wines and luxurious dinners bring no warmth or release of fellowship.

The wine–cellars of large houses and inns often extended under neighboring buildings; Thackeray speaks of a wine–vault that undermined an adjacent chapel. "There is an old monastery crypt under Garraway's (I have been in it among the port wine)," Dickens noted in 1860. Splendid residences might be connected underground to slum dwellings, and their rich stores of wine to sewage conduits or graveyards. In *Bleak House* such underground linkages symbolize the ultimate interdependency of the social classes, and the buried secrets of human passion they share. It is the lawyer Tulkinghorn, himself a vault of aristocratic secrets, who discovers the secret of Lady Dedlock:

> Mr. Tulkinghorn sits at one of the open windows, enjoying a bottle of old port. Though a hard–grained man, close, dry, and silent, he can enjoy old wine with the best. He has a priceless binn of port in some artful cellar under the Fields, which is one of his many secrets. When he dines alone in chambers, as he has dined to–day, and has his bit of fish and his steak or chicken brought in from the coffee-house, he descends with a candle to the echoing regions below the deserted mansion, and, heralded by a remote

### MADEIRA AT "THE WOODEN MIDSHIPMAN"

Symbolic of affectionate solidarity, Sol Gills' ancient Madeira is raised in a toast to Walter Gay's embarkation on the "sea of life" as a junior clerk at Dombey's import-export house in The City. The mellow old wine soon goes to their heads and they regale themselves with tales of famous shipwrecks over an order of steaks sent round from a nearby tavern.

reverberation of thundering doors, comes gravely back, encircled by an
earthy atmosphere, and carrying a bottle from which he pours a radiant
nectar, two score and ten years old, that blushes in the glass to find itself so
famous, and fills the whole room with the fragrance of southern grapes.

His closely kept cellar-key, and the opened bottle of wine, reappear symboli-
cally when Tulkinghorn is murdered.

MANNERS AND CVSTOMS OF Yᵉ ENGLYSHE · IN · 1849 ·   Nᵒ· 32·

Yᵉ VVYNE VAVLTS · AT Yᵉ DOCKS   SHOWYNGE A PARTYE TASTYNGE·

An obligatory stop on the itinerary of visitors to London and young gentlemen-about-town was
the wine vaults under the great warehouses on the London Docks, where tasting parties, drawing
samples directly from the casks of Sherry and Madeira and Port, could be arranged by tipping a
caretaker, with the customary result sketched above by "Dickie" Doyle.

In "No Thorofare" a "cellaret," or ornamented wine cooler, is described as "sarcophagus–shaped," while the wine-merchant who had owned it has "retired into another sarcophagus." Joey Ladle, the cellarman in the same story, complains of being "molloncholly" as a result of remaining so long in "a low dark cellar and a mouldy atmosphere," where a loathesome blood–red fungus hangs from the stone arches. But a visit to sample the hogsheads of wine stored in the great vaults under the docks of London was one of the prime tourist attractions of the last century; and more than one visitor came away fuddled.

In *Edwin Drood*, Dickens' last, unfinished novel, Mr. Jasper takes a wicker bottle with him when he accompanies Durdles the stone–mason to the cathedral vaults by night; and when Durdles is drunk (or drugged), Jasper explores the locked–up recesses of the ancient crypt, searching perhaps for a hiding-place for Edwin's body. There is also Mr. Grewgious, a lawyer who had made a dowdy bargain with life in his meagre chambers in Furnivals' Inn, but who also holds "some not empty cellarage at the bottom of the common stair." It is a phrase which echoes with overtones of Dickens' private life; he had lived in young–married days in Furnival's Inn; his marriage had proven a poor enough bargain emotionally, and he and his wife Catherine had separated in 1857. Since that time Dickens had maintained a liaison with a young actress, Ellen Ternan, which being secret may have seemed as though it were "at the bottom of the common stair" to the novelist. From his cellar, at any rate, Mr. Grewgious brings up

> . . . bottles of ruby, straw–coloured, and golden drinks, which had ripened long ago in lands where no fogs are, and had since lain slumbering in the shade. Sparkling and tingling after so long a nap, they pushed at their corks to help the corkscrew (like prisoners helping rioters to force their gates) and danced out gaily.

Dickens may be mingling in his memory many a southern wine he had enjoyed, a reminiscence made poignant by his failing energies and the likelihood that he would not again visit lands, real or imagined, "where no fogs are."

**Charles Dickens'
Cold Cups**

During his second tour in 1867–68, Dickens was entertained by his American publisher, James T. Fields, and his wife Anne at their home in Boston, where he obliged his host and hostess and their guests with cold cups prepared by his own hands. At their daughter Kate Fields' request, the novelist copied out his recipes and gave them to her. We offer them here, exactly as he wrote them.

**Cider Cup**

"Put into a large jug, 4 or 6 lumps of sugar (according to size) and the thin rind of a lemon. Pour in a *very little* boiling water, and thrust a napkin into the top of the jug so as to exclude the air. Leave it to stand ten minutes, and then stir well. Add two wine–glasses of sherry, and one–wine glass of brandy. Stir again. Add one bottle of cider (poured in briskly) and one bottle of soda water. Stir again. Then fill up with ice. If there be any borage, put in a good handful, as you would put a nosegay into water. Stir up well, before serving."

**Champagne Cup**

"Put into a large jug, 4 good lumps of sugar, and the thin rind of a lemon. Cover up and stir, as above. Add a bottle of champagne, and a good tumbler and a half of sherry. Stir well. Then fill up with ice. Borage as above. Stir up well, before serving."

**Moselle Cup**

"4 good lumps of sugar, and the thin rind of a lemon, as above. Cover up and stir, as above. Add a bottle of (still) Moselle, and a tumbler full of sherry. Then, ice as above. A few springs of wild thyme, or of jasmine, are a better seasoner for this delicate cup than borage. Stir well, before serving."

**Claret Cup**

"4 or 6 lumps of sugar, as before; give the preference to 6.

The thin rind of a lemon, as above. Cover up and stir, as above. Add a wine glass of brandy, then a bottle of claret, then half a bottle of soda water. Then stir well and grate in nutmeg. Then add the ice. If borage be used for this cup, half the cider cup quantity will be found quite sufficient. Stir well, before serving."

### Note

"The best substitute for Borage is a strip or two of the rind of a fresh cucumber. But it must not be left in the cup *more than ten minutes*, or its taste will be too strong. It is easily taken out with the spoon, as it will probably lie on top of the ice. None of these cups should be made more than a quarter of an hour before serving. *Never pour out of the jug, without first stirring.*

CHARLES DICKENS
His mark"
*Harper's Monthly Magazine*
144 (May, 1922), 719

(Borage is now commonplace in nurseries and garden shops.)

*Badminton Cup*    *1 medium cucumber, peeled; 4 oz. powdered sugar; juice of 1 lemon; 1/2 wineglass Curaçao; 1 bottle claret; 1 bottle soda water, iced; grated nutmeg.*

Combine in a bowl all ingredients save the soda water. When the sugar is thoroughly dissolved, pour in the soda water, add ice, and it is ready for use. Add a couple of sprigs of borage before serving.

*Bottled Silk*    Combine in a bowl a bottle of hock or Moselle, a half pint of Sherry, not too much peel of a lemon, two tablespoonsful of sugar, and a sprig of verbena. Mix well, ice, and serve.

*Reform Club Spiced Wine*

At the Reform Club wine was drunk in the old–fashioned English way. Sherry, Port, and claret preceded Champagne, but were served continuously throughout the meal. Spiced wine was a specialty of the club: a bottle of Sherry was poured into a deep pitcher placed in an ice–pail. Added were some maidenhair fern, a cup of strong green tea, a glass of soda water, some powdered cinnamon, cloves, and lemon peel. In hot weather ice was added. Made with Sherry it was called Sangris, and with claret Sangorum.

*Sherry Cobbler*

*2 tsp. powdered sugar; 2 or 3 small pieces lemon; crushed ice; 2 wineglasses Sherry; 1 tbsp. brandy; 6 strawberries.*

Into a tumbler three-quarters full of crushed ice put sugar, Sherry, brandy, and lemon. Pour back and forth between a second tumbler to mix. Add strawberries and drink through a straw. Provide a long–handled spoon to get the strawberries.

*Mastodon Cup*

*1 bottle very dry Champagne; 1 pt. soda water; 2 liqueur-glasses Curaçao; juice of 1/2 lemon; 1 wineglass brandy; a little powdered sugar.*

Combine in a bowl all the ingredients, stir well, add ice, and serve.

*Claret Cup*

*A little powdered sugar; 2 sprigs borage or cucumber peel; 1 bottle soda water, iced; 1 bottle claret; 2 wineglasses Sherry; 1 wineglass Maraschino.*

Combine in a large cup, pitcher, or bowl the claret, Sherry, maraschino, and sugar. Add ice. Just before serving pour in chilled soda water and add 2 sprigs of borage.

Burgundy Cup      *1/4 lb. powdered sugar; 3 wineglasses pineapple syrup; 1*
*bottle soda water, iced; 1 sprig borage; 1 bottle red Bur-*
*gundy wine; 1 wineglass Noyau; 1 wineglass brandy.*

Combine in a bowl or pitcher the wine, Noyau, brandy,
syrup, and sugar. Ice. Add cold soda water and borage just
before serving.

Minted Sherry     Into a bottle of good dry Sherry put about two dozen
tender young shoots of sweet spearmint, and let them remain steeping for a few days until their flavor is prominent.
Then pour off the Sherry into another bottle, discard the
mint, and keep for future use. Minted Sherry was a frequent
ingredient in Victorian wine cups in place of plain wine.

Hypocras          The grandfather of all English wine compounds was the
medieval Hypocras, for which we offer the following recipe:

*5 fifths of good red wine (9 pints); 1 lb. honey; 2 1/2 oz.*
*cloves and cinnamon; 1 oz. ginger; 2 oz. star anise; 1/6 oz.*
*saffron; 3/4 oz. cardamom.*

Crush the herbs and spices and add, with honey, to the wine.
Let the mixture stand for one year, then filter out the spices
and discard. Bottle the liquid for later use. Do not be
alarmed if it doesn't clear completely. Serve as an aperitif or,
heated, as a punch.

# Chapter Ten

# *"American Sensations"*

Dickens had a poetic vision of England as it had been: a Maypole Inn of warmth, comfort and accord among men; but he sometimes found it cheaper to live on the continent, and more profitable to visit America (twice), where he had heavy book sales and lucrative reading engagements. "I resolved to go to America—on my way to the Devil," says Charley in "The Holly–Tree" (1855). The gradual continentalization of English convivial tastes made the artist in Dickens grave, and their later Americanization would have appalled him. But as a man–of–this–world he enjoyed iced French wine, kept a good cellar and, as to the "American Sensations," he called them "meritorious drams" and "rare drinks." Thus he weathered the passing of Old England.

Horrified to discover that the blue–sky land–development scheme in which he had invested his little all is nothing more than a malarial swamp near what is now Cairo, Illinois, Martin Chuzzlewit returns to his rude hut in despair:

> "I wish you would pull off my boots for me," said Martin, dropping into one of the chairs. "I am quite knocked up. Dead beat, Mark."
>
> "You won't say that to–morrow morning, sir," returned Mr. Tapley; "nor even to–night, sir, when you've made a trial of this." With which he produced a very large tumbler, piled up to the brim with little blocks of clear transparent ice, through which the one or two thin slices of lemon, and a golden liquid of delicious appearance, appealed from the still depths below, to the loving eye of the spectator.
>
> "What do you call this?" said Martin.
>
> Mr. Tapley made no answer; merely plunging a reed into the mixture— which caused a pleasant commotion among the pieces of ice—and signify- ing by an expressive gesture that it was to be pumped up through that agency by the enraptured drinker.
>
> Martin took the glass, with an astonished look; applied his lips to the reed; and cast up his eyes once in ecstasy. He paused no more until the goblet was drained to the last drop. . . .

"This wonderful invention, sir," said Mark, tenderly patting the empty glass, "is called a cobbler. Sherry cobbler when you name it long; cobbler when you name it short."

This American scene is one of the more pleasant souvenirs of Dickens' first trip to the New World, in 1842. After a fearsome crossing, during which Dickens exerted himself to keep everyone's spirits up by inventing new drinks and games, Charles and Catherine Dickens set out to travel by "coach, steamer, wagon, prairie, lake and river" into "the Far West—into the Bush—the Forest—the log cabin—the swamp—the Black Hollow—and out upon the open Prairies . . . ten thousand miles or more." In the course of their journey they felt themselves to have been "beset, waylaid, hustled, set upon, beaten about, trampled down, mashed, bruised, and pounded by crowds." Dickens was thus given the treatment America has devised over the years for international pop stars, of whom he was one of the earliest. An "Address to Boz" in the New York papers warned him:

> They'll tope thee, Boz, they'll soap thee, Boz;
> Already they begin.
> They'll wine thee, Boz, they'll dine thee, Boz;
> They'll stuff thee to the chin.

They did; the bills of fare at such "Dinners to Charles Dickens" as that given at Papanti's Hall in Boston were staggering. Even Brillat–Savarin had approved American ingredients and cuisine, for the new nation's friendship with France had been a boon to wine–lovers and gourmets alike. One could probably eat and drink as well in New York in the forties as anywhere in the world. The wines available (but not their excellent quality) can be estimated by a contemporary satire on the typical Dickens dinner:

> Chateau Margaux de Cidrebaril
> Clos de Vougeot de Smalbiere
> Sillery Mousseux de Cornstalk
> Johannisberger de LaFontaine
> Haute Sauterne de Townpump
> Ale du Pere Adam.

It was hardly Dickens' fault, of course, that these festivities in his honor were so splendidly liquid, but he was blamed for the hoopla nonetheless. He had managed to offend several segments of the American citizenry by his remarks

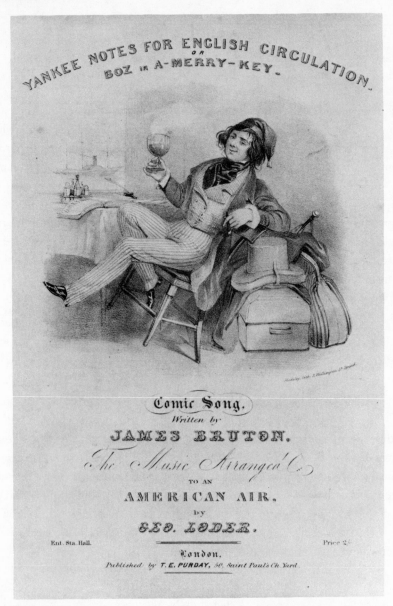

This cover of the sheet-music for a popular song designed to capitalize on the public interest generated by Dickens' first visit to America in 1842 sufficiently attests to the enormous trans-Atlantic popularity the novelist had achieved in the six short years since the serialization of *The Pickwick Papers* began. The visit soon turned sour, however, after the novelist criticized many cherished American attitudes and institutions, not least of which was the piracy of his and other English authors' works. It was to be another fifty years before the United States joined the International Copyright Convention.

on American literary piracy and on the Temperance Movement. Teetotalers branded him a boozer; his complaints about Temperance hotels led the Women's Temperance Movement to ban his novels; a phrenologist inspected his cranium at long range and pronounced him an "over-drinker." It was said that his "espionage" in America was floated on "juleps and cobblers," and that "he over-ran the whole country as though it were a tavern, and every large city a bar-room . . . all was barren—save where they . . . allowed him as much brandy and water as 'CD Esquire—and lady' might have occasions for." The outcry became paranoid: " . . . we suspected,—from a certain knowing leer of his eye, when we saw him sucking a sherry cobbler through a straw—that he was laughing in his sleeve at our folly. . . . " Indeed he might have laughed at the Bostonians who could not decide whether to fête him with wine at a stag dinner, or to invite the womenfolk and forgo the wine. Dickens was voluptuary enough to have wished for both if they had asked him.

It would not have assuaged American wrath to know that Dickens drank very little at such affairs. "Parties—parties—parties—of course, every day and night," he wrote home from Baltimore, " . . . but I am careful not to drink hardly anything and not to smoke at all." He took toast-and-water or a little Champagne in his glass, quietly replenishing it during the evening with soda-water. Still he seems to have sampled most of the American drinks then going, and he was as intrigued with them as his countrymen were soon to be also.

The early colonials were not "Americans," of course, but transplanted Europeans, who made the drinks they were familiar with at home from the materials at hand. Once fruit trees were planted, the English made cider, perry and "peachy," while the French made brandies. From New World grains the Germans brewed beer, the Dutch made gin and the Scotch-Irish made whisky. If Dickens had visited a New England inn in the eighteenth century he would have been pleased to find that his own favorites were very popular: in 1729 the usuals were punch, "flipp," rum, strong beer, brandy and cordials, metheglyn (mead), cider, and "cider royale," a distilled cider. Besides imported Sherry and Madeira, there were good wines and cordials made from native fruits and berries. "Cherry Bounce," sassafras mead, and foxgrape shrub were made as well as beers from parsnips, beet-tops, persimmons, pumpkins, ginger, and from the twigs and bark of birch, spruce and sassafras.

Thoreau's "men of Concord," if they were drinkers at all, were rum drinkers. New England rum was widely available as a result of the West Indian and African trade in molasses, rum, and slaves, and it entered into a variety of experimental mixtures—for the first American melting-pot was the landlord's

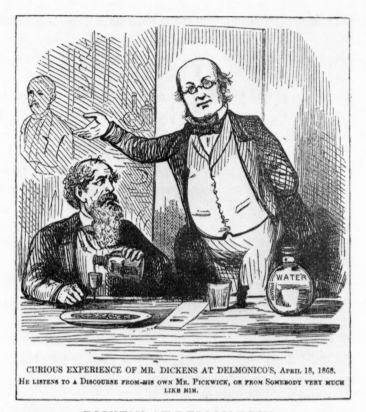

CURIOUS EXPERIENCE OF MR. DICKENS AT DELMONICO'S, April 18, 1868.
He listens to a Discourse from his own Mr. Pickwick, or from Somebody very much like him.

## DICKENS AT DELMONICO'S

Dickens and the American public buried the hatchet during his second tour in the winter and spring of 1867–68, when he gave readings from his own works to packed and cheering houses. A fine actor, he realized $25,000 from his American tour. The climax of the visit came at a magnificent banquet in his honor at Delmonico's in New York City, with Horace Greeley, who resembled Mr. Pickwick, in the chair. Evidence of Americans' continued belief in Dickens' intemperance may be found in the invidious contrast between the novelist, who is depicted filling his glass with spirits, while Greeley is fronted with a virtuous carafe of water.

mixing bowl. Rum–and–cider was the "Stone Wall"; rum–and–beer made "Calibogus" (or simply "Bogus"); rum–and–molasses was "Black Strap"; "Mimbo" or "Mim" was rum, sugar, and water, while "Switchel" was compounded of rum, vinegar and water.

Even "The Inimitable," as Dickens liked to style himself, would have quailed at the quantities of spirits consumed in colonial times. In 1785 an assembly of eighty people was said to have drunk seventy–four bowls of punch, eight bottles of brandy, eighteen of wine, and some cherry brandy—at the ordination of a minister! Meals were floated down with cider, beer or white wine, but the main dish signalled the appearance of Madeira, which was drunk in quantity by the men during and after dinner. "Toasts are drunk, cigars are lighted, diners run to the corners of the room hunting night tables and vases which will enable them to hold a greater amount of liquor. Sometimes dinner is prolonged in this manner far into the night, but finally the dinner table is deserted because of boredom, fatigue or drunkenness," wrote a French sojourner, Moreau de St. Mery. All in all, it has recently been estimated, Americans' per capita consumption of hard liquors in the early years of the last century averaged 9½ gallons annually.

Cider, or "gumption," normally ran about 6% of alcohol, and everyone drank it, including children. Farm–workers were forever downing tools to take a pull from the jug at the master's expense (and so charged, at the haymowing they would mow down everything in sight, trees and all). Cider distilled into brandy, or concentrated into "cider royale" by freezing the water out of it, was everywhere familiar as "applejack," "Blue Fish-hooks," or "Jersey Lightning," the latter owing to the many orchards in that state.

Liquor of all sorts flowed freely on the canal–boats on which Dickens and his wife travelled, where the men on board all had "foul linen, with yellow streams from half–chewed tobacco trickling down their chins." In fact, it seemed to St. Mery that "drink was the dominating idea"; and he noted that the price of a bottle of porter was the fine for getting into your berth with your boots on. In southern America the smell of raw whiskey was everywhere, according to Mrs. Trollope, to whom it appeared that men took their drams without ceremony or conviviality, seldom sitting down together. Whisky was twenty cents a gallon, and its ravages were obvious among slaves, the working–classes, drifters, politicians, journalists, and former members of the armed forces.

The Five Points slum in New York reminded Dickens of Seven Dials in London, being thick with grog–shops where children as well as adults drank spirits and talked the shop of their low trades, fencing, peddling, rag–and–bone picking, and prostitution. Not surprisingly, Temperance was one of the earliest of American reforms. When Dickens sailed for America in 1842, Father Matthew of Cork in Ireland had only just completed his astounding efforts, which resulted in cutting spirits–drinking in that country by half in only a few years

## THE FRONTIERSMAN

The English stereotype of the American pioneer takes his ease on barrels of "corn squeezin's," pistol in hand, picking his teeth with a Bowie knife, and remaining unruffled by the sight of a lynch-mob indulging in a popular outdoor sport of the backwoods. Bourbon whiskey takes its name from Bourbon County, Kentucky, where in 1789 Elijah Craig, a Baptist minister, hit upon the idea of putting the distillate of a largely corn mash into newly charred oak barrels, thereby imparting to it its characteristic color and flavor.

(1838–1842); but he had not begun his mission to England. Dickens had not yet seen Temperance to any extent triumphant, though he had mocked its fumblings. But in the United States the Washingtonian Temperance Society, founded in 1840, was at the height of its shortlived success; and while Dickens was in "the beautiful city of Cincinnati," a large and well–behaved Washingtonian parade went by his hotel, with bands playing, flags flying, officers on horseback and several thousand marchers. He thought the banners were very well painted:

> the chief feature . . . was a huge allegorical device, borne among the ship–carpenters, on one side whereof the steamboat. Alcohol was represented bursting her boiler and exploding with a great crash, while upon the other, the good ship Temperance sailed away with a fair wind. . . .

Dickens was less pleased with his short stay at a Washingtonian hotel on the way to Columbus, Ohio; for he wanted his wayside tot of brandy and couldn't get it. When sociability was offered of the true Pickwickian sort, he gladly entered into the spirit. In St. Louis he went on a prairie picnic:

> We had brought roast fowls, buffalo's tongue, ham, bread, cheese, butter, biscuits, sherry, champagne, lemons and sugar for punch, and an abundance of ice. It was a delicious meal, and as they were most anxious that I should be pleased, I warmed myself into a state of surpassing jollity; proposed toasts from the coachbox (which was the chair); ate and drank with the best; and made, I believe, an excellent companion to a very friendly companion-able party.

Everywhere he was pressed to sample what to him were novel mixed drinks. The Sherry Cobbler, which we have already met, was becoming the rage in London in 1842, along with that new dance sensation, the polka. The dialect of Dutch America seems to have supplied the name: a "cobble" was a lump or a stony hill—in this case, of broken ice. When young Chuzzlewit is introduced to one Major Pawkins—" 'One of the most remarkable men in our country, sir!' "—he holds the private view that the Major

> . . . could hang about a bar–room discussing the affairs of the nation, for twelve hours together; and in that time hold forth with more intolerable dulness, chew more tobacco, drink more rum–toddy, mint–julep, gin–sling and cock–tail, than any other private gentleman. . . .

Dickens delighted in rehearsing this exotic nomenclature, which would later sweep Europe. One of the men Dickens most wanted to meet in America was Washington Irving, an anglophile who had influenced the Dickensian fancy for jolly old English Christmas, cosy inns, churchwarden pipes and smoking bowls of Wassail. The meeting took place in Dickens' New York hotel room:

" 'What will you take,' " cried the enthusiastic Dickens, " 'a mint–julep or a gin–cocktail?' " (Irving had used the name "cocktail" as early as anyone, in 1809. Nevertheless, the origin of the term remains lost in the darkest jungles of etymology.)

Queen Victoria's chef, M. Francatelli, deigned in 1860 to recognize only the "Brandy Cocktail" among American drinks: "Put three lumps of sugar into a tumbler with a dessert-spoonful of essence of Jamaica ginger, and a wineglassful of brandy; fill up with hot water." This is really what the Americans were calling a "toddy." Both cocktails and toddies seem to have been equated in London with the warm "Morning Draught" of Pepys and the "Early Purl" of Dickens; they were often taken as "Eye-openers" and "Antifogmatics" in America, where drinking began with getting up in the morning. "Cocktails are compounds very much used by 'early birds' to fortify the inner man, and by those who like their consolation hot and strong," one of our sources writes in 1869. And Leo Engel, the reigning authority at the Criterion Bar in London in the seventies, recommended the cocktail for sporting parties, although he says he has heard of " 'weary sufferers' who take it in the morning as a tonic." He doffs his cap to the Americans, in any case, for "their ingenious inventions that have greatly added to the comfort of the human race," mentioning among many others the "Alabama Fog–cutter," the "Connecticut Eye–opener," the "Galvanic Lip-Pouter." Dickens mentions the Eye-opener, and would have enjoyed the rest; but Engel neglects to supply the details of their construction. By 1895, when the Davies brothers compiled their *Drinks of All Kinds*, a wide variety of American drinks were popular in London; both the Martini and the Manhattan appear, as well as a cocktail made with Bourbon whisky. All cocktails by then were served with lots of ice (much of which was also imported from New England), and sometimes gum arabic or maidenhair fern was added to make them syrupy in the English manner.

Juleps were recorded with high approbation by Captain Marryat in his book on America (1839). Varieties were made with claret and Madeira, but the mint julep of the South was the Captain's favorite. It required a dozen tender shoots of mint, upon which was put a spoonful of sugar and equal portions of peach and common brandy, so as to fill the tumbler about a third; the balance was crushed ice. "Epicures rub the lips of the tumbler with a piece of fresh pineapple, and the tumbler itself is often encrusted outside with stalactites of ice," wrote the enthusiastic Marryat, in an oft–quoted paragraph—but it is a too–sweet recipe. The best Virginia juleps were based on rye or brandy, while the less fortunate used moonshine. After the Civil War, Bourbon was all anyone could afford for

## CHAMPAGNE AT *THE ROWDY JOURNAL*

Colonel Diver, Jefferson Brick, and Martin Chuzzlewit share the "people's drink," Champagne, the potation of "new men" and *arrivistes*, in the offices of *The Rowdy Journal*, an American yellow sheet. The development of Champagne by Dom Pérignon in the seventeenth century had to await the invention of glass bottles and wired corks sufficiently strong to resist the gasses formed in the bottles by the working residual sugars. Before carbonation, the still white wines of the region were called Sillery, whence Syllabub.

his "greens and whiskey," which was rather too often taken as an eye-opener. Dickens was served a mint julep and a Sherry Cobbler at a Virginia plantation, and found them "never to be thought of afterwards, in summer, by those who would preserve contented minds."

The Sling (from Low German *slingen*, to swallow) was a tall iced drink, of gin usually, with bitters or lemon juice, water, and sugar; Dickens frequently served Gin Slings later in England. The Tom–and–Jerry, made with hot rum and water sweetened, spiced, and beaten up with eggs, was popular in both countries. It enshrines the names of Pierce Egan's famous sporting figures from a work, *Life in London* (1821), which in some measure prepared the way for Dickens' *Pickwick*. Perhaps because he was touchy about such matters, Dickens never mentioned the drink.

In a theater bar in Boston, Dickens encountered "Sangarees," "Timber Doodles," and other "rare drinks." Sangarees were then made with Port, Sherry, brandy, gin or even ale, with citrus fruit and ice in a tall tumbler: Dickens somewhere mentions a "sugarcane sangaree." The usual meaning of "timber doodle" was (and still is) the woodcock; perhaps someone invented a "woodcocktail." Dickens had reason to remember the drink, for American friends gave him a dog named "Timber Doodle," which lived to an advanced age and spent its declining years sitting in the Dickens kitchen with its ear apparently nailed fast to the door. And the name reappears obliquely in *Martin Chuzzlewit*'s Mr. Snittle Timberry. As for the other "rare drinks" mentioned above, they may have included: the "Spider" (gin, lemonade and ice); "Stone Fence" (whiskey, cider and ice); "Ribs" (cognac, gum arabic and shaved ice); "Ching Ching" (rum, sliced orange, peppermint, cloves, sugar and ice); "Asses Milk" (rum and sparkling lemonade); "Season Ticket" (cider, lemonade, sherry, orange–flower water, mint, sugar and ice); and "Hailstone," "Hailstorm," or "Snowstorm" (spirits with ice in various forms).

These were the drinks that took the later–Victorian world by storm under the heading in butlers' manuals of "The American Sensations"; the word is indicative of what had happened in England during the century. It was not strength alone that made the American drinks "sensational." Europeans were familiar with straight spirits, after all, than which nothing was stronger; Daniel Quilp with his Schiedam gin or boiling rum would have found the New World drinks effete. The Martini, for instance, began life as the "Martinez," said to be so named in honor of the San Francisco bartender who invented it: half sweet Old Tom gin, half red Vermouth, a little gum syrup and orange bitters, and a

## AN EARLY AMERICAN TAVERN

At a tavern in Charleston, South Carolina, circa 1760, Peter Manigault (seated left with his hand on a bottle) tells his inquiring friend Howarth across the table that the "tost" is with him. This effort to preserve a semblance of order is doomed to defeat, however, as the gentleman at upper left lustily renders "Hail to the Midnight Hark a-way." His oblivious neighbor toasts "Success to Caroline G-d dam[nm]e," while the two men at the upper right corner take wine together: "This one bumper Isaac," to which Isaac replies, "I shall be Drunk, I tell you Major." "Squire Isaac," cries the guest at the foot of the table, "your Wig, you Dog," which indeed he is twirling on a stick. The sober artist, George Roupell (lower left), interposes: "Pray less noise Gentn"; but the order of events is hopelessly confused. The negro servant is asleep in the window-seat and the parrot wishes he were. This lively sketch proves the enduring and trans–Atlantic nature of punch-taking after supper, a practice which the Pickwickians and the Bath footmen follow in detail—and with the same results.

lot of shaved ice. But punch and Negus and flip smacked too much of fusty assembly balls, where the old money made the new money feel uncomfortable, while straight drams of spirits were too crude, too low–class. To down a dram was to be shot from, or by, a cannon. Referring to a successful military engagement against some natives, Kipling in "Fuzzy–Wuzzy" boasts, "We sloshed you with Martinis," meaning not the cocktail but the new high–powered, quick–action rifle carried by imperial soldiers; but the pun was intended, and testifies to the reputation for potency of the drink.

Negus was a slow coach; but the Brandy Cocktail combined velvety going with speed of arrival that readily chimed in with that other combination of luxury, novelty, democracy, and speed, the railway. England gave the world the locomotive, but America created the "Locomotive Cocktail." "Sleeper," "Thunderbolt," and "Lightning" were names shared by cocktails and trains, while the "Highball," of course, was taken from the railroad signal meaning "a clear, fast road ahead." A man on his way up drank cocktails and rode the trains, and what is more, so did his lady. "I once overheard two ladies talking," writes Marryat, "and one of them said, 'Well, if I have a weakness for any one thing, it is for a mint julep.' A very amiable weakness, as Sam Weller would say, and proving her good sense and good taste. They are, in fact, like American ladies, irresistible."

They drank the "Saratoga Brace-up," "Mississippi Punch," the "Rocky Mountain Cocktail," the "Alabazam," "Monongahela Cobbler," the "Flash of Lightning," the "Morning Call," the "Rattlesnake," and in other dimensions of liberation and adventure, the "Office–Seeker's Consoler," the "Maiden's Blush," and the "Bosom Caresser." It is a little disappointing to realize that the last was merely a Grundyism for "Belly Warmer."

Many years later, in the Jazz Era, P.G. Wodehouse took a similar delight in the names of cocktails, which by that time were naturalized on both sides of the Atlantic: "Pink Pick–Me–Up," the "All Quiet on the Western Front Cocktail," "Annie's Night Out Cocktail," and "Gore–and–Soda" (taking after the Dickensian "Flesh and Blood"). The immortal "Lizard's Breath," familiar to all Eggs, Beans, and Crumpets, contained a dash of peppermint, an ounce of peach bitters, three dashes of Curaçao, and two-thirds of an ounce of brandy (as served at the Savoy in the 1930s). Yet Wodehouse also shows us Bertie Wooster revived by an egg beaten up in Sherry, just as Dickens would have recommended. The Angler's Rest still serves the old coaching drink, rum and milk. And when "Oofy" Prosser, the richest member of the Drones Club, goes "out on the tiles," the problem next morning would seem to have been the claret, which was still a favorite in the days of malacca canes, Buffy–Porson Two–seat-ers, nightclubs like "The Blotto Kitten," and "oojah–cum–spiff."

To Victorians the tall cocktail glasses were very appealing, as Dickens had found, covered with a hoary congelation, tinkling with ice, decked with cool mint or fruit slices, yet harboring sufficient strong spirits within to make a sort of glacial furnace. New England lakes such as Wenham and Walden were regularly stripped of their ice for export: "Thus it appears," wrote Thoreau, "that the sweltering inhabitants of Charleston and New Orleans, of Madras and Bombay and Calcutta, drink at my well." But in 1842 the ready availability of ice in America was a revelation to Dickens. "Hark!" he wrote in *American Notes*, as though alerting his countrymen to their destiny, "to the clinking sound of hammers breaking lumps of ice, and to the cool gurgling of the pounded bits, as . . . they are poured from glass to glass!"

Dickens was overjoyed to get back to England, where he wrote up his trip in terms that seriously offended his American hosts. A dozen years later, however, he made small amends in "The Holly–Tree," a reminiscence of many inns he had visited, including American hotels: "Again I drank my cobbler, julep, sling, or cocktail, in all goodwill, to my friend the General, and my friends the Majors, Colonels, and civilians all; full well knowing that, whatever little motes my beamy eyes may have descried in theirs, they belong to a kind, generous, large–hearted, and great people."

And this was the mood in which he made his second trip to the United States, in 1867–8. Both visitor and host country were less rambunctious as a result of their respective trials. In "an out of the way place" called Syracuse, however, Dickens noted that the hotel wine–list included "Mooseux, Aba-sinthe, Curacco, Annise and Margeaux." His tour–manager, George Dolby, tried the "Mooseux" while Boz essayed the "Table Madeira." They turned out to be one wine at different prices, and none of it drinkable. "There was nothing under three dollars a bottle," wrote Dolby, " and as the brandy (Jersey Lightning) was impossible, we had to fall back on our own flasks and small travelling stock. . . . " Good English gin was hard to find, but Dolby oblig-ingly went out by tug to the *Cuba*, a Cunard ship anchored in Boston harbor, and brought back twenty–four bottles which were added to Dickens' private stores at the Parker House. Scotch whisky was rare as well, but there were still discoveries to be made and old American acquaintances to be renewed. The Brandy Cocktail was "a highly meritorious dram," Dickens decided.

As we have seen, Dickens' services as a punch–compounder were much in demand, especially at the home of his American host, James Fields of Boston, where the poet Longfellow was an intimate. "No witch at her incantations could be more rapt in her task than Dickens was as he stooped over the drink he was mixing," wrote Longfellow; it was understood that Dickens' punch recipe was one he had from his father. As Dickens later wrote to Fields, who presumably wished to make it himself,

> Rash youth! No presumptuous hand should try to make the punch except in the presence of the hoary sage who pens these lines. With him on the spot . . . the daring mind may scale the heights of sugar and contemplate the depths of lemon. Otherwise not.

Dickens' reading tour was enormously successful, but it put a heavy strain on the writer, who suffered much from fatigue, sleeplessness, and an unshakable cold. He took counsel with the authorities in a New York bar, where they made him up a "Rocky Mountain Sneezer," which appeared to be compounded of "all the spirits ever heard of in the world, with bitters, lemons, sugar and snow. You can only make a true Sneezer when snow is lying on the ground."

> I cannot eat . . . [he wrote home] and have established this system; at seven in the morning, in bed, a tumbler of new cream, and 2 tblesp.ful of rum. At twelve, a sherry cobbler and a biscuit. At three . . . a pint of champagne. At five minutes to eight, an egg beaten up in a glass of sherry. Between the parts . . . beef tea. At quarter past ten, soup and anything to drink that I can fancy. . . . I am tremendously "beat". . . .

Two years later, in 1870, Dickens died of a stroke at his home near London, Gadshill; the principal cause was over-work. "Too much drink," suggested his American (and other) enemies. "Too much going to America," wrote his friend John Forster.

*Mint Julep*

> Behold this cordial Julap here,
> That flames and dances in his crystal bounds,
> With spirits of balm and fragrant syrups mixt.
>
> MILTON, *Comus*

There is little doubt that the Dickensian julep was made with a sweet fruit brandy, of which the closest modern equivalent may be Southern Comfort. What follows is a typical Victorian recipe for it:

Put into a large tumbler or cocktail shaker 2 1/2 teaspoonsful of water, a tablespoonful of powdered sugar, and two or three sprigs of fresh spearmint pressed well into the sugar and water until the flavor of the mint is extracted. Add 1 1/2 wineglasses of excellent peach brandy. Fill a glass with fine chopped ice and pour the mixture over it. Draw out the sprigs of mint and insert them stems downward in the ice, making a little bouquet of the leaves. Arrange berries in season and small pieces of sliced orange on top in a tasteful manner, dash with Jamaica rum and dust with powdered sugar. Sip through a straw or a stick of macaroni.

To H. L. Mencken, for whom "A man who puts rye whiskey in a Mint Julep would put scorpions in a cradle," the recipe above would have been anathema; and Bourbon-loving Kentuckians who "never put a horse in the stable hot, always slice their ham thin, and *never muddle mint*" view it with alarm. A proper Mint Julep is made in the following manner:

Fill a small coin–silver or other metal tumbler with crushed ice and dust very liberally with powdered sugar. Pour in good Bourbon to within an inch of the rim. Add more crushed ice so that the Bourbon cannot be seen. Stuff two or three sprigs of fresh young spearmint (not peppermint) together into the cup by the rim. In the midst of the mint place a straw cut to the length of the mint. Dust lightly with powdered sugar. (The point of a Mint Julep is to smell the mint while drinking the Bourbon.)

### John Collins

*(Thought to be an English inven-
tion, the brainchild of John
Collins, a barman at Limmer's
Hotel, London.)*

Put into a large tumbler or cocktail–shaker the juice of a lemon, a tablespoonful of powdered sugar, a wineglass of gin, and a tablespoonful of water. Fill two–thirds full with crushed ice, shake well, and strain into a glass. Fill up with soda water while stirring. Place two lemon slices on top and insert a couple of straws.

### Rocky Mountain Sneezer

Combine in a tumbler half a wineglass of Jamaica rum, a dash of brandy, a quarter wineglass of Maraschino, and a handful of new-fallen snow. Shake well and strain into a glass. Fill up with Champagne while stirring, then place a slice of lemon on top.

### Victorian Manhattan

Put half a wineglass each of red vermouth and whiskey in a large tumbler or cocktail-shaker and add thirty drops of gum syrup, ten drops of Angostura bitters, and six drops of Curaçao. Put in a little shaved ice, shake well, and strain into a wineglass. Put a bit of lemon peel on top.

### Port Wine Sangaree

In a tumbler two-thirds filled with shaved ice combine 1 1/2 wineglasses of Port and a teaspoonful of sugar. Stir well and grate nutmeg on top. Serve with slices of lemon stuck to the inside of the glass.

### Tiger's Milk

*1 small wineglass applejack; 1 small wineglass peach brandy; 1/2 tsp. essence of spice (nutmeg, cinnamon, gin-ger); 1 egg white; 1 tsp. powdered sugar; 1/2 tumbler milk; grated nutmeg.*

Combine in a tumbler the applejack, brandy, and spices. Beat separately the egg white with sugar and add it to the above, stirring. Fill up the tumbler with shaved ice, shake well, and strain into a glass. Add the milk and dust with grated nutmeg. (Equal parts of cider and Irish whisky were often substituted for applejack.)

**Rum Booze**

*8 egg yolks; sugar; grated nutmeg; 1 bottle white wine; 1 glass Sherry; 1 piece cinnamon; grated rind of 1 lemon.*

Beat the egg yolks well with some sugar and a grated nutmeg. Grate the yellow rind of a lemon on a piece of lump sugar, and put that, with the cinnamon and white wine, into a saucepan. When the wine boils take it off the fire immediately. Pour the cold Sherry into it and place in a pitcher, then pour it gradually into the egg mixture, whisking the while. Sweeten to taste and pour the mixture back and forth between two pitchers until smooth. Serve hot in a tankard or pot.

**Saratoga Brace–Up**

*1 tbsp. powdered sugar; 12 drops each of Angostura bitters, lemon juice, and anisette; 6 drops lime juice; 1 fresh egg; 1 wineglass brandy; Vichy or Appollinaris water.*

Combine in a large tumbler or cocktail-shaker the sugar, bitters, lemon and lime juice, anisette, egg, and brandy. Half-fill with shaved ice, shake thoroughly, and strain into another large tumbler. Fill with bottled water and serve.

**Whiskey Smash**

In a tumbler put half a tablespoonful of sugar, a tablespoon of water, and a wineglass of Bourbon. Fill two-thirds with shaved ice and add two sprigs of spearmint.

**Bosom Caresser**

Put into a small tumbler a wineglass of Sherry, half a wineglass of brandy, the yolk of an egg, two teaspoonsful of powdered sugar, and two grains of Cayenne pepper. Add shaved ice, shake well, strain, and pour into another tumbler. Dust with grated nutmeg and cinnamon.

Corpse Reviver      Put a third each of Maraschino, brandy, and Curaçao into a liqueurglass, being careful not to mix the colors. (One late-Victorian authority advises that if the corpse be a personal friend, he would eliminate the Maraschino.)

Mississippi Cocktail      Combine in a large tumbler or cocktail shaker a wineglass of brandy, half a wineglass each of Jamaica rum, Bourbon, and water, and a tablespoon of icing sugar. Nearly fill with shaved ice, shake well, and strain into a tumbler. Decorate with slices of lemon and orange and some berries in season. Serve with a strainer spoon or a straw and an iced-tea spoon.

Alabazam Cocktail      Combine in a tumbler a teaspoon each of Angostura bitters, sugar, and lemon juice, two teaspoonsful of Curaçao, and half a wineglass of brandy. Shake well with crushed ice and strain into a claret glass.

Office–Seeker's Consoler

*("If you have been haunting the President and the White House, day and night, for three months without success—take the consoler's beverage. Initiate the President into the mixing and you will get any office you like to ask for.")*

Combine 1 1/2 jiggers (ounces) of rye, a dash of Curaçao, fresh milk, and some ice in a tumbler. Stir and drink.

Sleeper      *1/2 pt. water; 6 cloves; 1/4 oz. cinnamon, bruised; 2 fresh eggs; 8 coriander seeds; 1 1/2 oz. sugar; juice of 1/2 lemon; 1/4 pt. old rum.*

Heat in the water all the ingredients except the eggs, which should be beaten separately in a basin. Pour the hot mixture slowly into the eggs whilst whisking. When well frothed, strain into a large tumbler.

# *Dickens' Cellar*

With the exception of a few insignificant odd lots, what follows is a list of the contents of Dickens' cellar at the time of his death. It is taken from the auction catalogue, carefully annotated with the prices received, that is now in the British Library. The auction, which included furniture and household effects, took place between Wednesday and Saturday, August 10–13, 1870, at Gad's Hill Place, Higham, near Rochester. The cellar was sold on the last day.

*Iberian Wines*

12 doz. brown Sherry, dry, golden (C.&G. Ellis, shippers)
 2 doz. Solera Sherry (Ellis)
 1 doz. Amontillado
13 magnums Golden Sherry, v. old, full flavoured, dry (Ellis)
almost 4 doz. rare old Madeira (Ellis)
 5 bottles 1818 Madeira
over 5 doz. 22-year old Port, v. dry & delicate (Cockburn)
18 magnums 1851 Port, v. dry
 5 doz. 1834 Port

*Claret*

16 doz. Medoc
 2 doz. La Rose
 3 doz. Chateau Margaux Bourjois [*sic*]
 5 doz. Leoville
 1 doz. 1858 Chateau d'Issan
 6 doz. 1858 Brane Mouton
 4 magnums 1858 claret

*Red Burgundy*

16 bottles Clos de Vougeot
17 bottles Volnay
 7 bottles Chambertin

*Champagne*

17 doz. Bouzy
 8 doz. Dry Champagne

*Various White Wines*

 2 doz. Moselle "Kuperberg"
 2 1/2 doz. Stein
18 bottles Sauternes
 3 1/2 doz. Hoch Johannisberg "Metternich"
 6 bottles Chablis
 5 doz. Chateau "y Quen" [*sic*] Bourgeois
 2 1/2 doz. Haut Sauternes

*Liqueurs, Cordials, Spirits, Whiskeys, etc.*

 1 bottle each Maraschino, Eau de Vie Dantzic, Chartreuse, Elixa de Spa, and
   Parfait Amour
 2 doz. 1854 Black Forest Kirschwasser
17 bottles Curaçao
 3 doz. Cordial Gin
 5 doz. Pine Apple Rum
over 10 doz. Dark Hennessey Brandy, 10 years old
18 doz. Pale Brandy (F. Courvoisier)
11 doz. Highland Whisky (Cockburn, Leith)
16 bottles Hollandche Genever Hoboken (deBie & Tarlay)

*Other*

 2 doz. cyder
12 doz. milk punch
30 bottles Australian red and white wines
 2 doz. sparkling muscatel

Dickens' cellar, of about 185 dozen bottles of various descriptions, realized 521 pounds, seventeen shillings and sixpence. It was commensurate with his station in life, the size of his household, and the scale of his entertaining, given the time in which he lived. It is not an ostentatiously large or rich collection, although there are several exceptionally fine vintages among the Ports, clarets, and Champagnes—the 1834 Port went for between six and seven pounds a dozen—but it is a very well chosen and representative group of wines within the limits of the taste of the day. Characteristically the Iberian wines (over 34 dozen), clarets (34 dozen), sweeter white wines (over 17 dozen), and Champagnes (25 dozen) predominate, and Burgundian reds and whites are slighted, though of these latter what he had is excellent. The "hard liquors" (about 53 dozen) are what one might expect to find in a cellar of that time.

But who drank the sparkling muscatel? We suspect it was Dickens' sister-in-law, housekeeper, and confidante, Georgina Hogarth.

# A Bibliographical Note

Since limitations of space will not permit us to list all of the scores of works we have consulted in preparing this volume, we will confine ourselves here to a brief selection of the most helpful.

The closest thing to a complete bibliography of works on drinks and drinking is A. W. Noling, ed., *Beverage Literature: A Bibliography* (Metuchen, N.J.: Scarecrow Press, 1971), which is conveniently cross-indexed. See also André Simon, *Bibliotheca Bacchica* (London and Paris: Maggs Bros., 1927) and *Bibliotheca Vinaria* (London: G. Richards, 1913). Simon is the author of dozens of volumes on every aspect of wines and spirits, including the authoritative *History of the Wine Trade in England*, 3 vols. (London: 1906–07; rpt. New York: Holland Press, 1964). The standard references on alcoholic beverages are Harold J. Grossman, *Grossman's Guide to Wines, Spirits, and Beers*, rev. Harriet Lembeck, 6th. edn. (New York: Scribners, 1977), and Alexis Lichine et al., *New Encyclopedia of Wines and Spirits* (New York: Knopf, 1974).

Among the hundreds of barbooks, butlers' and housekeepers' manuals, and cookery books published during the last century, we have relied mainly on the following: J. Davies, *The Innkeeper's and Butler's Guide*, 8th. edn. (Leeds: G. Wilson, 1868; but cf 5th. edn. 1808); "Bacchus," *Brewer's Guide for the Hotel, Bar, and Restaurant* (Norwich: St. Giles Printing Works, n.d.); "An Experienced Servant" (J.B. Davies), *The Butler* (London: Houlston and Stoneman, 1855); William Terrington, *Cooling Cups and Dainty Drinks* (London and New York: G. Routledge, 1869); Leo Engel, *American and Other Drinks* (London: Tinsley, 1880); Frederick and Seymour Davies, *Drinks of All Kinds* (London: J. Hogg, 1896); "Nathanial Gubbins" (Edward Spencer), *The Flowing Bowl* (London: G. Richards, 1899); and Anon., *Cups and Their Customs* (London: John Van Voorst, 1863). Delightfully pedantic is Charles Tovey, *Wit, Wisdom, and Morals, Distilled from Bacchus* (London: Whittaker, 1878). Among cookbooks we recommend Eliza Acton, *Modern Cookery in All Its Branches* (London: Longmans, 1845); but see the more available Elizabeth Ray, ed., *The Best of Eliza Acton* (Harmondsworth: Penguin, 1974); Isabella M. Beeton, *The Book of Household Management* (London: 1859–61; rpt. London and New York: J. Cape and Ferrar, Strauss, and Giroux, 1968); and C.E. Francatelli, *The Cook's Guide and Housekeeper's and Butler's Assistant* (London: R. Bentley, 1861—but it reflects a much earlier period).

There are innumerable books treating various aspects of food and drink in Dickens' life and works and in the Victorian period generally, among which we may note the following: Arthur L. Hayward, *The Days of Dickens* (London: Routledge and Kegan Paul, 1926; rpt. New York: Archon, 1968); B.W. Matz, *The Inns and Taverns of Pickwick* (London: C. Palmer, 1921) and *Dickensian Inns and Taverns* (London: C. Palmer, 1922); T.W. Hill, "The Dickens Dietary," serially in *The Dickensian* beginning with vol. 37 (Summer, 1941); Ian Watt, "Oral Dickens," *Dickens Studies Annual*, 3(1974), 165–81; William Ross Clark, "The Hungry Mr. Dickens," *Dalhousie Review*, 36(1956), 251ff; Margaret Lane, "Dickens on the Hearth," in Michael Slater, ed., *Dickens 1970: Centenary Essays* (New York: Stein and Day, 1970), and *Purely for Pleasure* (New York: Knopf, 1962); and Barbara Hardy, "Food and Ceremony in *Great Expectations*," *Essays in Criticism*, 13(1963), 351–63. Angus Wilson, *The World of Charles Dickens* (London: Secker and Warburg, 1970) is both handsome and reliable; and Geoffrey Fletcher, *The London Dickens Knew* (London: Daily Telegraph, 1970) complements Hayward.

The social history of drinking is well covered by William Younger, *Gods, Men, and Wine* (London: Wine and Food Soc. and M. Joseph, 1966), and S.B. Lucia, *Alcohol and Civilization* (New York: McGraw-Hill, 1963). Alec Waugh's *In Praise of Wine* (London: Cassell, 1959) repays reading.

More narrowly focussed on the nineteenth century are: Mrs. C.S. Peel, "Homes and Habits," in G.M. Young, ed., *Early Victorian England, 1830–1865* (Oxford: Oxford University Press, 1934); Elizabeth Burton, *Early Victorians at Home* (London: Longmans, 1972); and J.B. Priestley, *Victoria's Heyday* (New York: Harper and Row, 1972). Brian Harrison's *Drink and the Victorians* (Pittsburgh: University of Pittsburgh Press, 1971) is definitive. On the evolution of the modern pub, see Brian Spiller, *Victorian Public Houses* (New York: Arco, 1973) and Mark Girouard, *Victorian Pubs* (London: Studio Vista, 1975).

Instructive Victorian discussions of the place of food and drink in their lives include George Dodd, *The Food of London: A Sketch* . . . (London: Longman, Brown, Green, and Longman, 1856); and John Dunlop, *The Philosophy of*

*Artificial and Compulsary Drinking Usage in Great Britain and Ireland* (London: Houlston and Stoneman, 1839). Though a Temperance tract, the latter is a mother-lode of information about Victorian drink and drinking customs.

Guides to London high- and low-life familiar to Dickens must begin with that rollicking Regency tour-de-force, Pierce Egan's *Life in London. . . ,* illus. I.R. and George Cruikshank (London: J. Virtue, 1821). Henry Mayhew's *London Labour and the London Poor* (London: 1851, 1862–63; rpt. 4 vols. New York: Dover, 1968) is the last word about the lives of the street people in the metropolis. Dickens himself gave G.A. Sala the idea for *Twice Around the Clock in London* (London: 1859; rpt. Leicester: Leicester University Press, 1971). Under the pseudonym of Percival Leigh, Richard Doyle wrote and illustrated the entertaining *Manners and Customs of Ye Englyshe in 1849* (London: Bradbury and Evans, 1849) and *Birdseye Views of London* (1864). Blanchard Jerrold's handsome folio, *London: A Pilgrimage*, illus. Gustave Doré (London: 1872, rpt. New York: Benjamin Blom, 1968) is an excellent survey of mid-Victorian life in London. A similar volume, Albert Smith, *Gavarni in London*, illus. Gavarni (London: D. Bogue, 1849), is worth looking at. Dickens' son and namesake, Charles Dickens Jr., produced two informative annual guides for many years: *Dickens' Dictionary of London* (London: C. Dickens, 1879–94) and *Dickens' Dictionary of the Thames* (1868ff; rpt. New York: Taurus, 1972).

Pending completion of the Clarendon *Works*, trustworthy complete editions of Dickens' *oeuvre* are not to be found, but the Oxford Illustrated Dickens and the Penguin series will serve most practical purposes. Anyone who comes into possession of the National Edition, B.W. Matz, ed., 40 vols. (London: Chapman and Hall, 1906–08) should count himself fortunate indeed.

Finally, for the benefit of indefatigable bibliographers of bibulosity, the following libraries, besides the British Library and the Library of Congress, house extensive collections of drink literature: those of the University of California at Berkeley and Davis, the Hurty-Peck Library of Beverage Literature in Indianapolis, Indiana, and the Wine Institute in San Francisco. Any institution with a school of hotel management, such as Cornell and Purdue, is also likely to have a sizeable collection.

*Addendum.* Only after this manuscript was in the hands of our publisher did we discover a little book, privately published in England, called *Drinking with Dickens*. Its author is Cedric Dickens, great-grandson of Charles, and it is available by writing to him at Green Pastures, Holton, Wincanton, Somerset, BA9 8AY, England (£6.50). We are pleased to note that our efforts supplement each other without serious overlapping.

# Recipe Index

# *Index*

## DICKENS' PINT POT

As Bob Sawyer astutely remarked, beer belongs in its "native pewter" pot, pint- or quart-sized, like this of Dickens, although in the middle ages leather mugs were commonplace. Egg and beer or wine mixtures, which were not attractive to look at, were also served in pewter pots. The introduction of the glass pint mug during Dickens' lifetime ended the popularity of dark, opaque brews like porter, which were supplanted by the lighter, clearer mild and bitter ales that by 1900 had come to dominate the trade.